HAY
y Gelli

SHOP
PUB

DESTINATION
HAY

Copyright © 2018 Great Little Destination Guides

www.facebook.com/GreatLittleDestinationGuides

ISBN 978-1-9996738-0-2

First published in Great Britain in 2018 by
Great Little Destination Guides

Printed in the United Kingdom by Orphans Press, Leominster
www.orphans.co.uk

We have made every attempt to assure the accuracy of all
entries in this guide. However things change frequently here as
elsewhere, so, sorry... but we accept no responsibility for any loss,
inconvenience or otherwise resulting from the use of this guide.

To keep in touch with what's going on, or just to speak to us
(we'd love to hear from you!) please contact us at
www.facebook.com/GreatLittleDestinationGuides. Thank you!

CONTENTS

HERE BE, NOT ONLY, HISTORY AND BIOGRAPHY, BUT ALSO, PROSE, POETRY, PLAYS, PHILOSOPHY, ART, ARCHITECTURE, MUSIC, EROTICA, ETCETERA, ALL PLACED WITH RESPECT TO THEIR PERIOD, THUS CREATING A RICH SEQUENCE OF CHRON-OLOGICAL LOCATIONS. ORPHEUS MEETS UP WITH MEDEA AGAIN. ARISTOTLE INSTRUCTS ALEXANDER. OVID SHARES THE STAGE WITH YOUNG JESUS. THE BARD RUBS SHOULDERS WITH DRAKE & BLAKE ADVISES PAINE TO LEAVE THE COUNTRY. GUIDES AND INTERPRETERS (HISTORICAL FICTION) ARE PLACED IN SOME RESORTS TO ASSIST YOU. TREAT THEM WARILY, THEY TOO HAVE IMAGIN-ATIONS. NEEDLESS TO SAY ALL CON-CEIVABLE DESTINATIONS ARE NOT AVAILABLE. BUT EACH DAY I DO SOME-THING TO 'RECTIFY THAT. (I BUY AT LEAST ONE BOOK) KEEP IN MIND! YOU CAN FIND THE BOOK, YOU CAN MAKE A CUP OF TEA, YOU CAN CLIMB BACK INTO BED. BUT IF YOU FAIL TO

SWITCH OFF TODAY

Conventional wisdom says that Hay-on-Wye should have been killed off by the online revolution. Conventional wisdom says these days there is no money in selling books, or indeed anything from 'bricks-and-mortar' shops. Conventional wisdom says a successful town of independent retailers, miles from a main road or railway station, is Pie-in-the-Sky-on-Wye.

But Hay doesn't do conventional wisdom, or conventional anything. People think differently here. The transformation from Market Town of the Marches to Book Town of the World began in 1962, with Richard Booth, a character whose egomania and surreal sense of humour was the toast of Fleet Street for decades. In 1977, King Richard, as he had by now become, announced that Hay would become independent from the rest of the UK. The revolution was televised and Hay thrived on it.

Bookmania aside, Hay has always been a special place. European refugees arrived here after the Second World War, then hippies in the Sixties; in the Eighties and Nineties, New Age Travellers bought a rave scene that was a foil for the burgeoning genteel crowds attending Hay Festival. Despite conservative rural roots, a large part of the Hay community has long held an independent, anti-Establishment credo, and for its diminutive size (pop: 1600), it probably has as many creative people living and working here as anywhere on earth. Today, Hay's writers and artists are being joined by a new wave of younger folk pursuing other creative and artisan lifestyles.

Yet if Hay's growth has been organic and free of the blight of so-called planners, there is no dispute that the town has been saved and made, in its current form, by two of the great British entrepreneurs of the late twentieth and early twenty-first century. Richard Booth founded Hay 'the Book Town', yet just as he was running out of viable ideas (and money), along came Peter Florence, who founded Hay 'the Book Festival Town'. Both have also successfully exported their ideas globally.

It's unusual for Richard Booth not to have the last word, but we think he'd agree with Peter Florence when he says "If you're interested in the world and in people, in love and death... and how to be happy, then Hay is a great place to be".

Ancient Hay-story

Although Hay has long been a disputed territory, owing to its position on the English-Welsh border, its early origins are mostly unremarkable. The Romans came and went without leaving much trace and although Anglo-Welsh hostilities date back to the 5C, Hay and the surrounding areas were spared the major battles and bloodshed of the pre-Medieval era. In fact it could be said that Hay did not really exist in any significant form until the arrival of the Normans.

Offa's Dyke

The most important early figure to leave his mark, quite literally, on the local landscape was King Offa of Mercia (757–796) who fought continually against the Princes of Powys in the second half of the 8C. Seeking to preserve the integrity of his Mercian kingdom – a great chunk of central England bordering Wessex and present-day Wales – Offa decided to construct an earthwork. His famous dyke, meaning trench or ditch in Middle English, roughly follows the present border, and originally comprised a ditch on the Welsh side some 88ft (27m) wide, with a rampart (earth mound) 8ft (2.4m) high on the English side. It ran for 177 miles, coast to coast, from Prestatyn in the north to Chepstow in the south, and must have provided quite an obstacle even if it was not defendable along its entire length. If nothing else it was a significant marker; according to some historians, the Welsh would hang every Englishman found west of Offa's Dyke, whereas the English would return any Welshman found on their side, minus his ears.

Today, less than half the dyke remains in any recognisable form (the greater part of this being well to the north of Hay), the rest has been ravaged by farming and the passage of time. The Offa's Dyke Path National Trail, opened in 1971, more or less follows the original course of the dyke. From the Brecon Beacons, it passes through the centre of Hay, runs along the north/west bank of the Wye for a short way, and heads towards Kington.

Norman Wisdom

It is said that when the Norman conquerors spread their attention west to the Welsh Borders from England, not only did they meet some of their toughest topographical challenges, but that the feisty Welsh also provided some of their fiercest opponents. The Norman method of conquest in the Marches was two-fold. Marcher Lords (effectively the rulers of the Welsh Borderlands) were created by authority of the king who allocated the Lords tracts of land on which taxes were levied. However, if a Lord took and held a piece of land across the border into Wales, then not only was it his to keep, it was also free of taxes. Of course this attracted a particularly mercenary warlike type, who would fight tooth-and-nail, not only against the Welsh, but also any fellow Norman knights looking to grab a piece of the action. Sometimes though, it was more prudent to do a deal with the enemy, intermingling Welsh and Norman/English blood in marriage, rather than spilling it in battle.

The Normans made Hay a strategic border fortification in the late 11C with the first Lord of Hay being Bernard de Neufmarché. The original Norman castle (*see p81*) was built c1100, just outside the present walls, and the fledgling town developed as a market centre. The adjacent Church of St Mary was dedicated in 1115.

The 'Great Gateway' of the Norman keep, thought to be the oldest working defensive gate in Wales.

The Ogre, Bad King John and the Giantess of Hay

As the 13C dawned, Hay passed to the de Braose family, a brutal dynasty favoured by King John. Their relationship deepened when (it is said) William de Braose witnessed the murder of the boy-prince and heir apparent, Arthur of Brittany, by order of his uncle, King John. Some say William himself may have been the killer. He certainly had form, already known as The Ogre after an infamous massacre of Welsh nobles, whom he had summoned to Abergavenny Castle in 1175 under the pretext of a truce. Whatever really happened, he was deeply implicated in the deed, and was probably given the three local castles of White, Skenfrith and Grosmont by King John, in return for his silence.

William's wife, Matilda (Maud) de St Valery (aka Moll Walbee), was no less a colourful character. Local legend has it that she was not only a Giantess, but built Hay Castle in a single day. In fact, Maud was probably just an exceptionally tall lady for her day, and the built-in-a-day myth may have owed something to its swift construction alongside her personal work on the castle gateway.

As William became stronger, John grew more nervous and also angry that his subject owed him large amounts of money. He threatened to take Maud's son, also called William, as surety, and the feisty Maud is said to have sealed the family's fate with the indiscreet words that "I will not deliver my sons to King John, for he foully murdered his nephew Arthur, whom he should have cared for honourably". The outraged king mobilised his army and imprisoned Maud and William junior. Some say they were walled up alive in Corfe Castle, Dorset, where they starved to death, others say they were held at Windsor Castle. William senior, now an outlaw, fled to Ireland, then to France, where he died soon after.

Ancient Names

Hay owes its name to its early overlords: the Norman French 'La Haie' means hedged enclosure, while the Welsh equivalent translates to Y Gelli *(uh gethli)* meaning grove, copse or wooded enclosure. Some purists suffix this to become Y Gelli Gandryll ('the grove of a hundred plots'). It did not become Hay-on-Wye until quite recently *(see p76)*. The word Marches derives from the Old English word mearc meaning border land.

This was not the end of the story as far as Hay was concerned, however, as his two brothers, Reginald and Giles, made an alliance of convenience with Prince Llywelyn the Great (the de facto King of Wales) against King John. In 1215, in retaliation, King John burned both Hay Castle and town.

Black William

There is a final twist in the ill-starred de Braose story. In the ever-changing alliances of the Marcher Wars, yet another William de Braose – son of Reginald, nephew of The Ogre – was captured by Llywelyn in 1228. Remarkably, although he was hated by the Welsh, who called him Gwilym Ddu (Black William), he was not only able to make peace with the Welsh king, but also cemented the bond by arranging to marry off his daughter, Isabella, to Llywelyn's son Dafydd. Within two years, however, William had very much worn out his welcome, caught in the bed chamber of Llywelyn's wife. In 1230 he was publicly hanged by Llywelyn, much to the delight of the 800 or so local spectators, many of whom retained long and bitter memories of the de Braose dynasty.

War and Peace

By 1231 alliances had again changed and Hay Castle was in flames once more, this time at the hands of Llywelyn after a particularly bloody battle down by the Wye, said to have cost the lives of some 300 English knights. Hay then passed to Eva de Braose, widow of the late (Black) William, and the Castle was rebuilt. Over the next century or so Hay was tossed to and fro, fought over by Anglo-Norman warlords and the descendants of Llywelyn. However, with the victory of Edward I over Llywelyn ap Gruffudd (aka 'Llywelyn the Last') in the Wars of Conquest, 1277–1283, Anglo-Welsh strife, as least as far as Hay was concerned, was greatly diminished.

In 1536 Wales and England united and the time of the Marcher Lords was finally over. Over the coming centuries Hay was to have many more dramas but none as eventful as its 13C baptism of fire. Perhaps, that is, until the arrival of 'King Richard' in the 1960s, but that's another story *(see p13-17)*.

The Folio Society

The Folio Society

Reading Room

Reading Room

RICHARD BOOTH

ght Anywhere in the

Richard Booth's Book Town: Making Modern Hay

As the 1960s dawned, Hay was in the doldrums. In 1962 the railway closed and thanks to new A-road construction elsewhere in the region, Hay had become even more isolated. Regional centres, such as Hereford, lured Hayites away with their work opportunities, and supermarkets in larger towns meant that Hay shops were shutting at an alarming rate. Even that mainstay of 1960s local entertainment, the cinema, had just closed. For visitors, there were just two hotels and one B&B. As Booth himself recalls, "When I started, the most prosperous part of the Hay economy was probably the fruit machine at the British Legion Club". Cometh the hour...

Chapter One

Born in 1938 and brought up in southern England, Richard George William Pitt Booth endured, rather than enjoyed, a classic upper-class education at Rugby School and then Oxford. Emerging as a self-confessed "third-class aesthete", he came to Cusop Dingle, a short walk from Hay, to live with his parents in Brynmelin, a rambling country house, where he still lives today. Persuaded by his parents to pursue a conventional career, he spent a short but unsuccessful stint as an accountant in the City of London, before returning to Brynmelin. Here he would indulge his passion – second-hand books – first stimulated when his father introduced the 14-year old Richard to a book dealer in Woking, Surrey.

With property prices at rock bottom, and with a private income inherited from his grandfather (a former director of Yardley perfumers), the budding young entrepreneur bought the former Fire Station in Castle Street as his first bookshop (see p32). It is still there today, marked by an old fireman's helmet (see p14). "Libraries purchased, any quantity from a single volume to a whole library", ran his advert in *The Western Mail*. A library was duly purchased (from the Archbishop of Cardiff), and the most valuable books were stripped out and sold on, to other dealers or through his own shop. Booth learned the trade quickly; one library followed another, then more. A single shop premises was soon insufficient and a warehouse in Hay became his second bookshop. Much of his stock came from academic institutions, moving away from the Classics, clearing out dusty ancient leather-bound volumes and in the process also discarding many treasures. "In Wales I could buy 1500 volumes for £3. Bala College Library was sold for a few thousand pounds; today it would fetch millions". Ironically some of Britain's new universities, such as Surrey, York and Hull, were eager to snap up Booth's newly acquired tomes. Other buying opportunities were afforded by cash-strapped country houses, and the 250-or-so working men's libraries in Wales (affiliated to mines, steelworks etc) which were closing.

Books came from all over the world. In Ireland's Cork Cathedral library, "undisturbed for nearly two hundred years, the fur of dust on the top shelves was so thick it was like touching a rabbit". Booth visited Australia, Canada and the USA and fell in love with the latter, returning there frequently, buying and selling Herculean quantities of books.

Boomtown

In 1963 Booth bought not only Hay Castle *(see p36)*, but a capacious agricultural warehouse in the centre of town, turning it into **Richard Booth's Bookshop** *(see p62-63)*. By 1965, his burgeoning empire needed even more space, so he moved to the biggest premises in town, the old cinema *(see p80)*, filling it with 250,000 volumes. It was for a while the largest second-hand bookshop in the world. During this period he also acquired a clutch of other Hay shops. Between 1962 and 1968, turnover had rocketed from £6,000 to £100,000 (in today's terms the equivalent of £90,000 to £1.2 million).

It wasn't just the boss who benefited. Once-empty Hay shops were now full of books, dealers and other customers. Hay began to attract visitors from all over the world and Booth became a celebrity, courted by the press and the Wales Tourist Board.

Most of the town became reliant, directly or indirectly, on his book-dealing expertise and Booth became famous in Hay for offering jobs to almost anyone he met. Even with his self-confessed "anarchistic attitude towards recruitment... I was able to turn an ex-miner, an ex-bishop and the daughter of a local cleaner into successful second-hand booksellers". In just a few years one man's unlikely vision had changed Hay's account from red ink to black.

Unfortunately this rapid expansion was, like the man himself, impulsive and largely uncontrolled; while Booth was a brilliant book dealer and self-publicist, long-term financial consequences were an unwelcome afterthought. Decisions were made on the hoof and often on a whim, which only added to his charisma. Meetings were usually conducted in the pub with copious quantities of alcohol and all manner of practical jokes. He surrounded himself with "famous and eccentric friends", none more so than April Ashley, Britain's first prominent transgender personality, who made the transition from merchant seaman to *Vogue* fashion model and international socialite.

Independence

In 1977 Richard Booth pulled off his greatest publicity coup, announcing that Hay was going to break away from the rest of the UK. On April Fool's Day the official Declaration of Independence was made. In the anarchic meetings that followed, it was suggested that, logically, Booth should become King of the new state – 'Richard Coeur de Livre' – and he remains King of Hay to this day. "My cabinet was picked in five minutes in the pub. MacKendrick, a Scottish stone mason, was appointed Minister for Scottish Affairs on account of his accent. There was a unanimous veto on having a Minister of Arts for fear of encouraging ponces. Norman Radcliffe had so much to drink he could not remember whether he was supposed to be Prime Minister or Minister of Defence." Among the many 'honorary' titles the king subsequently doled out, was 'Duchess of Offa's Dyke' to April Ashley. Down by the Wye, the 'Hay Navy' comprised a rowing dinghy with a piece of drainpipe, in which gunpowder was ignited to give a royal salute. The proclamation was followed by the new 'Hay National Anthem', *Bridge Over the River Wye*, a remix by Mike Oldfield *(see p104)* of the *Colonel Bogey March (see p77)*. The king's crown jewels comprised a lavatory ballcock for an orb, a copper pipe (from the methane gas industry) for a sceptre, and a crown, whose red jewel centrepiece was salvaged from the collar of a dead poodle found by the side of the road.

The news of Hay's Independence spread quickly across much of the world and bought millions of pounds-worth of publicity and visitors. A Hay passport, edible (rice paper) currency of the 'Free State of Hay', bumper stickers and more were to follow.

In 1978, on the first anniversary of Independence, Hay Day celebrations were staged. *The Hay Herald*, the 'national newspaper' (now defunct) was launched with the headline '*Hay Quits EEC*' – (the EEC being the former name of the European Union).

A Charismatic King

He was simultaneously inconsistent and logical, gentle and outrageous, self-serving and selfless, brilliant and banal, but not for a second was he boring. And I was ready to believe him.

Journalist and writer, Vitali Vitaliev, on meeting Booth in 1999.

Ahead of his Time...

Among all the tongue-in-cheek tomfoolery, Richard Booth's Hay Home Rule manifesto, articulating the frustration he felt that national government was ignoring the plight of decaying market towns like Hay, was remarkably prescient.

Democracy does not exist; it has been strangled by bureaucracy... (citing the demise of public transport and waste of tourist board money in Wales)

Everything superior is made locally – the new kingdom of Hay must be famous for the uniqueness of its products...

The decline of rural areas is not inevitable if we take our destiny in our own hands.

Booth goes Bust

Meanwhile, back in the real world, while second-hand books continued to arrive in Hay in prodigious numbers, the account books were telling their own story, of over-stocking, over-staffing and illiquidity. Despite this, the King ploughed on, visiting the USA even more regularly than before. In 1983 the *Guinness Book of Records* described Richard Booth as "the world's largest second-hand bookseller [with] 9.9 miles of shelving and a running stock of 900,000 to 1,100,000 books". It might also have added that by now he was bankrupt.

In 1982, a rival had come to Hay, determined either to destroy or rescue the financially strapped Booth, whichever your viewpoint. Leon Morelli's first act was to buy the Hay Cinema Bookshop, the most profitable part of Booth's empire. In the process, according to Booth, Morelli stole his most able lieutenant (Derek Addyman, *see p57*) and also 'gazundered' Booth by £10,000. It was the first battle in a war between the two that would go on for some 15 years. As Booth's star waned, Morelli went from strength to strength, buying The Swan Hotel, The Crown Hotel (now occupied by The Old Electric Shop) and Kilverts Hotel.

A new Hope

In 1981, just as Booth was made bankrupt, salvation arrived in the shape of Hope Stuart. He would later say, "A Kentucky heiress bailed me out." Hope would prove to be the perfect partner in every sense, organising both his business and personal affairs. They wed soon after and are still married today. The King's other love affair, with the USA, was also rekindled, and during the 1980s he imported over one hundred 20-ft containers, each containing around 400 boxes of books.

International Booktowns

"By 1990," lamented Booth "there were almost no libraries left to buy", and although business still flourished, the great buying sprees were over. The King of Hay turned his attention to his next major project, International Booktowns. At its simplest, the aim was, and still is, to spread the Hay model of second-hand bookshops being at the heart of, and reviving small rural communities. The first partnership, formed with Redu, in Belgium (pop. 400) was a great success, and today, 15 second-hand book and comic shops serve both the community and 200,000 visitors per annum.

In 1995 however, even the indefatigable King Richard had to take time out when a brain tumour "the size of a cooking apple" was discovered. The operation could well have killed Booth, or left him brain-damaged. Today, the left side of his face is still partly paralysed, but his brain remains sharp, and he continues to pursue his Booktown passion. On April 1st 1998 he was once again crowned at the castle, this time 'Emperor of all the World's Second-hand Book Towns'. At the last count there were 19, along with three more prospective members (www.booktown.net). The empire now stretches from Iceland to New Zealand, across mainland Europe to South Korea and Malaysia.

By the Millennium, thanks largely to the drive and enthusiasm of Richard Booth (and helped in no small way by the Hay Festival), Hay had become well established as one of the most popular visitor attractions in Wales. In 2004 Booth was awarded the MBE for services to tourism.

In Hay itself, however, his empire has all but disappeared. In 2007, his flagship, Richard Booth's Bookshop was sold and in 2011 the King departed from his castle to his 'country palace' at Brynmelin. Booth's last shop in town, The King of Hay (see p33), is set to close in June 2018.

Hay Festival

For many people, Hay-on-Wye is 'Hay-the-Festival', and vice-versa. But the two are very different, as anyone living or trading in town will tell you. One is new books, one is old books; one is 11 days a year, the other 365 days a year; one is the icing on the cake, the other the bread and butter on the plate. The majority of Hay folks welcome the Festival, though it's undeniable a few begrudge its here-and-gone celebrity nature, particularly since it moved to the outer residential part of town. Whatever the opinions, nearly everyone would agree that the thought of Hay without its famous Festival is...well, unthinkable.

In the Beginning

The genesis for the festival was the Florence family. Norman Florence, who was Sam Wanamaker's first manager at The Globe Theatre in London, and his actress wife, Rhoda Lewis, had recently moved to Hay, and decided to hold a festival. They were aided and abetted by their son, Peter, who had recently graduated from Cambridge and was just back from touring the world with a show based on the poetry of Wilfred Owen. Fortuitously, so it is said, Peter had just won a sum of money in a poker game and threw this into the venture: "There wasn't a vision," says Peter. "The idea was, let's make it fun, let's throw a party and invite some mates around, but it soon got out of hand".

The first Hay Festival was staged in 1988 comprising 33 events; most performers were friends of the Florences, It was held in various venues around the town including the back bar of the British Legion Club, St Mary's Church, and the Baskerville Hall Hotel, Clyro Court *(see p120)*. A steward at the latter recalls a terrible storm during a performance by a steel band. "In no time a small river was going through the tent. People sat on their chairs. Then they stood on their chairs. Sheets of music flowed past. And still the band played on." Despite such mishaps, that first festival attracted 4000 people.

The Word Spreads

The following year, Peter Florence persuaded the great American playwright, Arthur Miller, to attend. The seed was well and truly sown and in subsequent years the festival spread to take over several locations in the centre of town, including the Church, the Castle and primary school, before eventually outgrowing all these and moving to a 20-acre site half a mile away on the edge of town.

A Festival of the Mind

The sea change came in 2001, the year when Bill Clinton appeared, though in fact it had much more to do with the foot-and-mouth crisis gripping the UK than the superstar speaker. Peter Florence: "A week before his arrival and the day after we'd shelled out the non-refundable six-figure fee for Clinton's first post-presidential lecture in Europe, there was a foot-and-mouth outbreak six miles down the road. We met with the NFU (National Farmers Union) to discuss the possibility of cancellation. They were adamant that we go ahead. They said farmers were on the rack, but the town needed the festival business and a bit of fun. Young farmers manned the washes and contamination pads. That was when the festival became owned by the community".

At the time Clinton's fee was regarded as an eye-watering amount but his famous line, describing the festival as "a Woodstock of the mind", has since been repeated so often, that in publicity terms, it has probably repaid the fee many times over.

Hay Festival Today

The festival "party" now features more than 500 speakers – including not only the most eminent and famous novelists in the world, but also the finest minds in the fields of science, politics, history and music – in over 800 ticketed events, spread over 11 days across dozens of marquees and meeting spaces attended by over 250,000 visitors.

In 2017 big names included Bernie Sanders, Gina Miller, Graham Norton, Jacqueline Wilson, Howard Jacobson, Garry Kasparov, Stephen Fry, Tracey Emin, Eddie Izzard, Yanis Varoufakis and Ken Dodd. Eclecticism is a festival byword. While these A-listers played to audiences of up to 1700 strong, paying between £7 and £30 per ticket, in side rooms and small tents, children's authors, illustrators and science teachers built quantum computers, engaged their young charges with the natural world, told tall tales, conjured magic, and much more, sometimes for free (in fact nearly 100 festival events are free). Somewhere in between, the majority of events featured 'other' writers and authors – some well known, some not – but each an expert in their chosen field, holding forth on all kinds of everything, at £7 per session. The great thing about Hay is that these can be just as rewarding and enlightening as talks by headline names. As former BBC political editor, Nick Robinson, puts it, "The joy of the festival is that it allows you to stumble across things you didn't know you wanted to know".

Festival Format

Hay, and indeed most other literary festivals, are unlike a typical three-day music festival which has an all-inclusive price, on-site camping, and go on from around noon until the small hours. The Hay Festival lasts for 11 days and each event is ticketed separately, with the most popular often selling out in advance. If you can't get a ticket for an event, however, you can go to the box office shortly before it is due to start and see if there have been any returns, which you can then pick up for the price of a charitable donation.

The day normally runs from around 10am–10pm, though there are some late-night events, and while there is no on-site camping, there are plenty of other options (including camping) very close by. One thing is for certain, you need to book accommodation months in advance.

While the spoken word is king, music is also an important part of the festival and in 2017 you could have caught a Craig Charles DJ set; international reggae and soul stars, Fat Freddy's Drop, from New Zealand; Will Young indulging his love of jazz; Khamira, fusing Welsh folk, Indian classical, rock and jazz, plus Radio 3 classical lunchtime recitals. Next year, and the year after that will be similarly eclectic.

The BBC are a perennial at Hay, broadcasting a live daily digest of speakers, musicians and personalities. These events are always free and well worth attending. Elsewhere there are high-quality refreshment tents, featuring local food specialities, *Hay Does Vintage* retro clothes and paraphernalia, local arts and crafts, an Oxfam bargain books tent, and much more.

The Festival Bookshop

Almost every event at the Festival is staged to promote a new book and immediately after the talk, eager fans form orderly queues at book-signing tables. The pop-up Festival bookshop hosts some 500 signings in 11 days, so manager Gareth Howell-Jones has seen his fair share of celebrity authors. His favourite tale stars, well... everyone's favourite – Henry Winkler, aka 'The Fonz'.

'HENRY WINKLER gave me a fiver!!' The expression of incredulous delight on the nine-year-old boy's face was enchanting. He had asked the actor, once 'The Fonz' and now the inspirational author of the Hank Zipzer children's series, for his autograph, apologising that he had no money to buy a book. Henry slipped effortlessly into his beloved 'Fonzie' mode and responded like a true hero, giving the child £5 to buy the book, then signing it. Heeeeey!

Not every author is quite so generous. "I don't sign paperbacks", Paul Elkington (Hay Festival Technical Director) remembers hearing Jeffrey Archer say grandly to a fan at the Festival. "You miserable b.....", muttered Elkington under his breath. Archer heard him and complained to Peter Florence. Whatever Florence said to Elkington remains private but Archer has never been asked back to Hay.

The Things They Say... At and About Hay Festival

Hay-on-Wye? Is that some sort of sandwich? Arthur Miller

...a Woodstock of the mind. Bill Clinton

In my mind it's replaced Christmas. Tony Benn

I don't do research anymore, I ask the audience at Hay. Ian McEwan

From the gardens of Bombay, all the way to lovely Hay. Ian Dury rewrote these lyrics to *Hit Me With Your Rhythm Stick* at the festival for one of his last concerts

With feminism, Al Qaeda, world music, iconoclastic sculpture, David Frost and Desmond Tutu all in the line up, the obvious gap was a burlesque bonkbuster. Dancer and author of *Tease*, Immodesty Blaize introducing herself in 2009.

Hay-on-Wye is way on high. The Hay-on-Wye fortnight holds a very special place in the book-lover's calendar. Ask any author or reader. This is the one we wrestle our diary into submission for... Stephen Fry, Festival President since 2014

You never know what to expect from the audience. The hecklers there are usually those who have had one too many glasses of elderberry champagne and they'll shout out a complicated literary point of order. Bill Bailey, musician and comedian

In 2001 Paul McCartney appeared. He was so boring. He said he'd been influenced by the poets of San Francisco, and when someone asked if he visited City Lights, its famous poetry shop, he said, 'I've never heard of it'. At the end of his talk, he upped and went, leaving behind 1,000 people who'd each paid £15 and wanted books signed. Derek Addyman (bookseller) on 'the disappointment of Sir Paul'

Hay is a Renaissance-style festival focused on solving humanity's problems through literature, science and philosophy; while Davos is a more technocratic affair...Hay is a richer experience and perhaps a more lasting one. Reuters

When Peter Florence asked me to become president of the Hay Festival; my first thought was that he must be joking or on psychotropic medication. This is the honour of honours... Stephen Fry

The most important literary festival in the Western world.
New York Times

Hay is the party to which everyone wants to be asked. Writers feel snubbed if they don't get an invitation, relieved when one arrives. It's like a vast country wedding, with the sensitivities to match.
Aida Edemariam, *The Guardian*

On stage, Debbie [Harry] and her Jazz Passengers had Hay whipped up into a genteel frenzy. It was going very well until one of them leant into the microphone and shouted: "Hello Hay, how many shepherds in the audience tonight?"
Rex Fontaine, *The Independent*

The Literature Festival has given people an additional reason to visit Hay and I cannot deny that mountains of dusty second-hand books can sometimes be boring.
After nine years of bitter opposition, Richard Booth, who once produced 'Arts, Tarts, Farts', T-shirts, referring to the Festival, grudgingly admits that it might not be so bad for Hay after all!

The Glastonbury of literary festivals.
Alice O'Keeffe, *The Guardian*

I was 39 or 40 before I'd heard of Hay. I could hardly get my head round the idea of a festival about books. My prejudices were terrible and then I went there to promote my autobiography and it was the coolest thing I'd ever experienced in my life; so many clever people, such a buzz.
Chris Evans

Q&A Hiccups

After the speaker has finished there is invariably a question and answer session with the audience. Sometimes it doesn't go to plan!

After Arthur Miller's lecture on freedom of speech, censorship in Eastern Europe and satire in the Cold War, the first question was, "What was she like?" (she being Miller's second wife, Marilyn Monroe). Miller just laughed, as did the audience.

When Joseph Heller was rebuked by an audience member, that after Catch-22, he hadn't written anything as good, he replied "No, I haven't, but neither has anybody else".

The Winter Weekend

In late November 1999 a pocket-sized version of the summer festival was launched. In 2017 the Winter Weekend celebrated its 18th birthday, with its biggest ever programme, including a new 450-seater venue and 70 speakers, starring Monty Don, Jeremy Vine and Matt Lucas. All Winter Weekend events take place in town. Associated festivities over the same weekend include switching on the town's **Christmas Lights**, **Hay Food Festival**, with over 50 stalls showcasing the very best of local produce, plus **Hay Does Vintage,** which transforms the Market Square into a festive outdoor flea market, featuring over 50 vintage and retro traders.

Today Hay, Tomorrow the World

The slogan of the festival is *Imagine the World* and, extending this maxim, Hay not only 'imagines the world', but has reached out to it over the years, exporting the festival name and ideas to 20 different countries, including Peru, Kenya, Bangladesh, Mexico, the Maldives, India, Lebanon, Ireland, Colombia, and Spain. In 2017 three-day literary festivals were staged in Aarhus (Denmark), Arequipa (Peru), Cartagena (Colombia, *pic opposite, top*), Queretaro (Mexico) and Segovia (Spain).

A rather less exotic locale is Parc Prison Bridgend, which has been staging **Hay in the Parc** since 2008; it is held simultaneously with the main festival, some 70 miles north. The aim of Hay in the Parc is to help change the lives of prisoners, their families, and in turn the impact of their crimes on wider society, thus giving the lie to the sometimes-criticism that Hay Festival is only ever concerned with elite liberalism and the 'chattering classes'.

On the (Brecon) Road

One of the nicest traditions of the Hay Festival is that many of the locals, along the stretch of the Brecon Road between the town and Festival, set up roadside stalls and gazebos, selling tea, coffee, home-made cakes, sandwiches and perhaps handicrafts. Moreover, proceeds often go to charity. Some also provide a mini-café facility in their gardens, giving festival goers the option of taking a (cheap) break from the main site and escaping the hubbub.

Oxford Road Car Park

There aren't many guidebooks that begin extolling the joys of the car park, but then again you won't visit many car parks with a glorious view like this. In fact it used to be the Castle orchard, which you'll appreciate better when you cross the road and see the back of the castle, through the tall trees.

Looking out across the fields, to the hills beyond, Offa's Dyke Path *(see p94)* runs alongside the left hand side of the car park and skirts Cusop, before rising up to Hay Bluff, then marching south.

The Craft Centre

One of the joys of Hay is that most of its shops, pubs and cafés are housed in ancient buildings bursting with character. So why are we suggesting you visit this modern 'carbuncle' for your first taste of Hay? For a start, sweet-toothed readers (and their children) wouldn't forgive us for missing out the Willy Wonkaesque joy of **The Fudge Shop**, which has been making its creamy sugary treats by hand on the premises for over 10 years. *www.thefudgeshop.co.uk. Open daily.*

Eirian, meaning 'bright, glowing, beautiful' in Welsh, is the apt name for **Eirian Studio Glass**, established and run here by Paul Edward Brown and Rowena Jane Lloyd since 1989. All the glass you see, bespoke lighting, contemporary hand-cut glass tableware and one-of-a-kind studio glass, is either made or cut on the premises. All glassblowing and glassmaking takes place outside shop hours, so you won't see Paul or Rowena in action, but you can take a full-day or half-day glassblowing course and try it for yourself; ask or see their website for details. *www.glassgallery.co.uk. Closed Wed & Sun and Bank Hols.*

With a New Age vibe that echoes Hay in the 1970s and 1980s, **Satori Designs** have been selling an amazing range of stones, gems and crystals plus wind chimes, candles, fantasy art and general 'magick stuff' for over 30 years. We like their jewellery, easily the biggest range in Hay. You can also channel your inner hippy next door at **OtherWorldz**. *Both open daily.*

Cross the road, and with the Tourist Information Bureau on your left, continue into The Backfold.

The Backfold

Hay's bookishly named Backfold (a bookbinding term for the inner margin of the folded sections) is a charming narrow alleyway with a quirky selection of shops, some of which snuggle right into the castle walls. Poke your nose into the first hole-in-the-wall-like space on the right and you'll discover the natural scents of **The Thoughtful Gardener**, run by Jacqueline and James Kennett, purveyors of practical but very stylish gifts for gardeners: Burgon & Ball Sophie Conran secateurs anyone? When it's time to wash those green fingers, try their own handmade Castello de Haye aroma-therapeutic soaps and botanicals range (named after the original Norman castle), made with water from the spring by the Old Castle, reputed to have healing properties. Most striking is the Black Mountain Charcoal Soap. www.thoughtfulgardener.com.

Nan Tiques and **Lot 51** are always worth a look for vintage and antique finds, the latter mostly for furniture, while **Haystacks Records** (*see opposite*) is crate diggers' heaven.

Turn left out of The Backfold onto Castle Street, go past Rohan and Castle Greengrocers.

The Great *English* Outdoors

When the stove is blazing and Boudica, the handsome docile wolfhound belonging to shop owner Athene English, is sprawled out in front, you'll feel as if you've intruded into a shoot for *Country Homes* or *Country Living* magazine. Which is quite possible, as the shop has been in both and regularly features in high-class lifestyle magazines. The friendly staff belie any formality or stuffiness, however and the collection of clothing, such as handmade tweed jackets and waistcoats made from (Fairtrade) yak's wool, traditional leather goods (Russian Reindeer if you really want to impress), stylish recycled accessories, gorgeous old and new Welsh wool blankets, plus eclectic 'traditionalia' (perhaps a beard brush or moustache comb for the man in your life?) all make this handsome late Georgian property a very homely place to browse or buy.

www.greatenglish.co.uk. Open daily.

Continue for a few yards and cross the road by The Blue Boar.

Legal Highs in Haystacks

A practical joker and shrewd marketeer in the true Hay mould, in 2016 owner Haydn Pugh put a sign in the window (of Haystacks Records) advertising 'Legal Highs sold here' – crucially, beneath the image of a vinyl record. The local constabulary were informed, failed to see the joke, marched into the shop and demanded the sign should be removed. When Haydn pointed out that the accompanying picture made it clear it was only a musical reference, and with no other legal highs on sale, common sense prevailed. Haydn 'admits' the resultant publicity did him no harm! He also tells of a customer who saw the sign and asked, "So where's the dope man?" "I'm talking to him!" Haydn replied.

With its crates of vinyl, '60s and '70s paraphernalia, music-related books and magazines, and a general unkempt hippyish vibe, Haystacks looks like it has been around for decades, but this is also down to clever marketing; "I've only been here seven years", says Haydn (before that he was a printer working largely for Richard Booth), "but I painted the shop purple and made it look like we've been here decades, you've got to put your own spin on it!".

Boz Books

Although this was not the first second-hand bookshop in Hay, this is where the story of modern-day Hay began, in 1962, when a 24-year-old Richard Booth bought the building that formerly housed the Old Fire Station for around £700. The town surveyor gave an old fireman's helmet to Booth who hung it outside the shop. It's still there, above a heavily weathered 'blue plaque'.

It was, in Booth's own words, an inauspicious start. In addition to selling books, he also sold antiques from here, though apparently without any great enthusiasm. *"What's this?" asked a customer, hoping for an explanation of a Chinese root sculpture. "It's thirty bob [£1.50]" I replied.* Business prospered however, and the rest – as they say – is 'Hay's-story'.

Today Boz is a classic Hay antiquarian bookshop with beautiful leather bound books, specialising in Dickens and 19C authors. Beware, the owner is looking to move away, so do check opening times. *www.bozbooks.co.uk. Closed Sun.*

Continue on this side of the road, past Red Indigo, be careful as you cross to Days Household Goods.

Style and substance

Castle Street is home to some very chic, not to mention some very useful shops, including **Days Household Goods** *(pic above)* where you'll find wooden 'sporks', handmade Portuguese ceramics, cute cookie cutters and cutting-edge workwear jackets. As you continue down Castle Street, you'll find stylish clothes, footwear, accessories, gifts and homeware in both the **Number Two** shops *(www.number-two.co.uk)* and, on the opposite side, in **Flow**.

The King of Hay

The last vestige of Richard Booth's once ubiquitous Hay Empire, the King of Hay bookshop is as eccentric as its namesake, home to an array of the King's personal outpourings, including his many pamphlets (eg. *Abolish the Wales Tourist Board...*) and Independence memorabilia. You can buy Dukedoms (£55), Earldoms (£50), Baronies (£40) or become a Knight or Lady of the Realm (£30), or for rather less you can own a Hay car sticker or passport. This is also the only place where you can get a hand-signed copy of Richard Booth's entertaining autobiography, *My Kingdom of Books*. Finally there is the 'Patriotic Machine' to experience. In the King's own words:

The subject kneels, puts [50p] in the slot and watches an inspiring scene pass before his eyes. While the [Hay] National Anthem plays, the Hay flag waves and a portrait of me in ceremonial dress is illuminated; my eyes flash red and a troop of [toy] soldiers fire. A white flag emblazoned with the words 'Bureaucrats Beware!' shoots out from a revolving turntable.

Sadly, in April 2018, the King of Hay announced that it was closing as from June 2018. Whether its stock and its aristocratic ennoblements will still be available online is unsure at time of writing. We hope that the Patriotic Machine will find a new home open to the public and that one day the town will open a museum that displays some of these curiosities.

Open Mon-Fri 10-12.30. www.richardkingofhay.com.

Cross the road

Addyman Annexe

This is the third branch of the town's famous retailer. Trading since 2002, the Annexe is, in the owners' words "the [Addymans] shop that specialises in the sexier material: beat, sex, drugs, art, modern firsts, poetry, philosophy, left-wing history and the occasional occult work". *The Antiquarian Book Review* called it "the Jewel in the Crown of Hay". We'd disagree only in as much as we think the original Addymans *(see p57)* is more compelling and much quirkier.

The eye-catching much-photographed *trompe l'oeil* beside the shop, depicting a rather furtive-looking 18C dandy, was commissioned by Addymans. *www.hay-on-wyebooks.com. Open daily.*

Continue on for a few yards and go through the arch to enter the castle precincts.

The Castle in 1797

Hay Castle

Hay Castle, the oldest, most dominant and most important building in Hay, is also one of its most enigmatic. Why is it a 'real castle' on one side and a Jacobean mansion on the other? Does the King live here? Who owns it? How did it become semi-derelict? And why on earth are there open-air 'bookshops' in its precincts? With its melancholic empty eye-socket windows, elaborate gables and rough-stone ruins silhouetted against the sky, it's a romantic, sometimes spooky place, and has been the backdrop and inspiration for many a tale.

In Days of Yore

Hay Castle was not the town's first fortification *(see p81)*, but it was probably the first stone castle, and was the rock around which the medieval town flourished.

Contrary to local lore, it was not built in a single day by a giantess, but over several decades by Norman warlords. Bernard de Neufmarché began its construction around the turn of the 12C and it was well established by 1188. The most famous castle builders were William de Braose ('The Ogre') and his larger-than-life wife, Matilda (Maud) de St Valery. For more on them and this period *see p9*.

Hay at this time was almost permanently in a state of flux, with rule passing between Norman/English and Welsh forces. The castle, ever in the firing line, was destroyed by King John in 1216, and again in 1231, by the Welsh prince, Llywelyn. It was soon rebuilt however, under the protection of Henry III, and in the following decade, walls were projected out from the castle, right around town, not only to defend it from two-legged aggressors, but against the packs of wolves that once roamed this area.

The next couple of centuries saw Hay once again passing to and from English and Welsh forces, though the castle remained largely unscathed. From the 15C onwards, relative peace descended on the region, and the castle began to transform from martial to domestic. The addition of the Jacobean mansion appears to have happened in two phases, c1580 and c1630. Since then, various local families (Boyles, Gwynnes, Vaughans, Baileys...) have more or less continuously occupied the castle as a private home. It was used as a vicarage for a while from 1825 onwards, as noted by Reverend Kilvert *(see p101)*. Unfortunately major maintenance or rebuilding was rarely undertaken and over time its fabric slowly deteriorated.

Recent Times: from Carousel Horses to Books

In 1939, the roof and much of the mansion accidentally caught light, in the process destroying one of the finest 17C oak staircases in the country. The castle was subsequently bought by Victor Tuson, who owned nearby Clifford Castle (also in ruins). He was married to a fairground heiress and for a time the castle suffered the indignity of being a store for fairground odds and ends. By 1963 it was in such poor repair that a local young book entrepreneur named Richard Booth *(see p13)* bought it for just £5000. "Behind its magnificent Norman walls I could shelter from my parents' objections to nocturnal female visitors and store as many books as I could buy". Painting a picture of its past neglect, Booth tells how he asked one of his workers, Frank English, to remove from a chimney a 14ft-deep jackdaw's nest, its enormity caused by twigs falling into it over many decades. "I played Beethoven in the fireplace below, very loudly (said Frank), it's the only way to get rid of them".

Booth attracted a motley entourage: "the castle became known as a drug-taking centre of sin", he admitted. In 1977 the castle was in flames again. As Booth relates it, he stacked the fireplace "with a great tree trunk" and then retired for the night. Unfortunately the 'tree trunk' refused to stay in the hearth, and Booth, woken by the sound of crackling, was fortunate to escape with his life. Nearly 80% of the building was severely damaged and, adding insult to injury, the fire revealed that the most historic surviving feature, its 25-ton oak central partition, was completely rotten thanks to centuries of damp. Repairs were made but Booth could not afford to do the job properly and although he continued to live here, the fabric was in a more perilous state than ever.

In 2011 Booth decided to put the castle up for sale and it was bought by the Hay Castle Trust (HCT). It was reported locally that it sold at, or near its £2m asking price. HCT has been committed to its renovation ever since, and work has just started on ambitious plans which include: a viewing platform in the Norman keep, offering fantastic views of the Wye Valley and the borderlands; re-opening the 'Great Gateway' of the Norman keep, to allow access from the town side; an exhibition space to display items from major national collections; a reading room and archive; spaces for educational purposes, meetings and talks; and a café set in the old coach house and stables.

Saved by the Belly

One of the strangest events in the castle's 900-year history happened during one of Richard Booth's drink-fuelled evenings, when an inebriated friend, Hugh Vickers, climbed to the top of the keep.

Stumbling drunkenly he fell into the portcullis shaft. The fall would have been 30 feet but the shaft narrowed and his body became wedged between the thick stone walls. Hugh's life was saved by his enormous stomach. The Hay Fire Brigade discussed his fate for an hour before he was finally extracted by a passing potholer.

The Castle Today

Looking at the castle from the Market Square, the earliest part is the **Norman keep**, to the left. Unfortunately it is unstable and unsafe for entry. Presently, though probably for not too much longer, you can walk, with care, around the bank and see the keep at close quarters. Its medieval wooden '**Great Gateway**' is thought to be the oldest working defensive gate in Wales. To the right of the keep is the east wing of the **Jacobean manor**, roofless and derelict, its decorated stone walls in a state of collapse.

Go through the gateway on Castle Street to the lovely green space below the castle featuring its famous open-air **Honesty Bookshop**, a tradition since the 1960s, initiated by Richard Booth. All books are £1. Pop your money in the collecting box - all proceeds go towards castle restoration (there is another Honesty Bookshop on the upper level, but this may be closed during castle renovations). At festival time, food and drink stalls set up here.

If you want to see inside the castle, join **Hay Tours** who meet weekly in the town square below the castle (*Thu 11am Apr–Dec; more frequently during Hay Festival*). You will see inside the surviving rooms of the roofed Jacobean section, learn the location of the dungeon – still in use as a gaol up to the late 19C – and much more. Outside, you'll be taken around the front of the Norman keep and the curtain wall, and shown some of the more recent discoveries about the Castle's history.

Tours cost £5 (which goes to the castle renovation fund) and are highly recommended. However, as work proceeds on the castle, access will inevitably be restricted.

www.haytours.org, www.haycastletrust.org.

The Magus

Hay Castle in Fiction

Hay has two local writers who vividly capture the romance, history, legend and supernatural potential of the castle. Both also interweave modern events, mysteries and crimes into the ancient fabric of the Marches.

The castle was moonlight-vast, all its ages fused together by the shadows, chimney stacks like the backs of hands turned black... writes Phil Rickman in The Magus of Hay (2013), his "darkish thriller" featuring the ongoing adventures of Merrily Watkins, a latter-day exorcist for the Diocese of Hereford.

www.philrickman.co.uk.

Barbara Erskine's debut novel, *Lady of Hay* (1986), has sold over two million copies, translated into some 30 languages. Its title refers to Matilda 'Maud' de St Valery *(see p9)*, who is the heroine of the story. Erskine's latest Hay blockbuster, *Sleeper's Castle* (2016) was a *Sunday Times Top Ten bestseller*. In 1977, Barbara, already known as 'Queen of The Time Slip', received the title 'Dame of the Kingdom of Hay' from Richard Booth.

www.barbara-erskine.co.uk.

Turn right out of the castle and cross Castle Street.

Mostly Maps

"I came here for a long weekend in 1978 and never left", says Kemeys Forwood, the owner of Mostly Maps, who, like many traders in town, started as a Richard Booth employee before setting up to sell antique maps and prints, with his wife Sally. Their stock-in-trade is striking antiquarian maps: including the first printed map of Shropshire (1577) and a World War II silk escape map, illustrative plates (many hand-coloured) and gorgeous antique OS maps *(pic opposite)*. Antique topographical prints, caricatures, and botanical prints are also specialities.

Aside from Kemeys and Sally, the two stars of the shop are the cartographic mannequins of 'Flora' and her smaller companion 'The Mapman'. Both are ingeniously clad almost entirely in maps.

www.mostlymaps.com. Closed Sun & Mon.

Hay-on-Wye Booksellers

Another former employee of Richard Booth, Michael Bullock began bookselling on a trestle table in The Swan Hotel. In 1972 this pair of classic 18C black-and-white buildings became vacant and Michael has never looked back. "In those days there were queues of book dealers outside here at 7.30am." While many customers may be lured in by the remaindered bargain books in the right-hand window, there are also thousands of older more valuable volumes inside. Some of the most precious sit in a glass case near the counter: eg. a signed first edition of *On the Black Hill (see p69)* at £850. Upstairs is a mini-labyrinth of rooms, corridors, nooks and crannies, piled high with thousands of books on all subjects.

Today, of course, bricks-and-mortar shops (or in this case timber-wattle-and-daub) are declining in favour of the internet, which is why Hay-on-Wye Booksellers have a huge warehouse just outside town. Here are two mindboggling statistics: only 0.25% of Hay-on-Wye Booksellers' total stock is actually held in the shop; they sell 30,000 books per week online all over the world.

And, in case you were wondering, the Egyptian Mummy 'sarcophagus' by the door is actually a bookcase.

www.hayonwyebooksellers.co.uk. Open daily.

The Drawing Room

This recent addition to the Hay art scene is a small funky modern gallery run by artist-owner Mark Harrell. Mark studied in London and New York where he specialised in Abstract Expressionism. During this time he lived in the near-legendary Chelsea Hotel, where his work hung on the walls. Mark is an expert on Buddhist art and has lectured in the V&A in London.

The space not only features Mark's productions but the works of local artists. Exhibitions change regularly.

www.thedrawingroomathay.uk.

Open only during exhibitions, Thu–Sat 10am–3pm.

Shepherds Ice Cream Parlour

'Balls to Walls. Eat Hay National Ice Cream' urged the anti-corporate, buy-local slogan, coined by Richard Booth, on Hay T-shirts in 1977. We'd love to tell you that this was the inspiration for Shepherds Ice Cream, which today is without doubt 'Hay's National Ice Cream', but unfortunately that's just not true, as Shepherds wasn't to be born for another decade.

In 1987 the pioneering Juliet Noble and Martin Orbach founded Shepherds, the country's first commercial producers of ice cream from sheep's milk. Their first five flavours were vanilla, strawberry, ginger, lemon and, erm... carob, they admit, rather sheepishly – albeit being ahead of their time! After several years selling at agricultural shows and local events, they opened their current shop, in typical Hay maverick fashion, on April 1, 2000.

Today they make 16 flavours, their best seller being Toffee Honeycomb. Other less usual flavours, available on a rotating basis, include Tayberry, Damson & Sloe Gin, Orange & Cardamom; Rhubarb & Custard. The queues here are legendary and on summer weekends snake down Castle Street. Shepherds also supply many of the major festivals up and down the country, including Glastonbury, and have been at every Hay Festival since 1989.

But is sheep's milk ice cream any better than the traditional stuff? With a fat content of less than 7%, it is around 5% less fatty than cow's milk ice cream, yet still achieves a smooth, creamy texture and a clean fresh taste, akin to a gelato. It also contains nearly three times the amount of vitamins and minerals. Initially viewed with suspicion, even derision, by early customers and critics, Noble and Orbach have had the last laugh in these health-conscious times.

www.shepherdsicecream.co.uk. Open daily. See also p116.

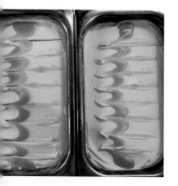

Raise a Cone to the King

In good weather you can sit outside, on the raised platform opposite Shepherds, to enjoy your ice cream. The modern statue on the wall high above is Henry VII, who has no discernible links with the town, but is the only English king to be born in Wales. There is of course a 'Welsh king' who was born in England, living just a couple of miles from here. For more on him *see p13-17*.

Continue down the hill and turn left by the Pharmacy onto The Pavement. You might like to browse for antiques and bygones at **Timeless Treasures***, but before you go back up the hill to explore the town's markets (see p45), continue two doors down.*

The Keeper's Pocket

It's not just hunting-fishing-shooting types who will enjoy browsing the antiques, oddities and vintage taxidermy selection in this shop, run by former gamekeeper and Wye ghillie, Rob Derrick: "It's all about provenance and history," he enthuses, recalling how the handsome head of Britain's most famous late-19C horse, Honest Tom, 'King of the Shires', once passed through The Keeper's Pocket. Rob's specialty is Victorian-era taxidermy and other natural history items, but other eye-catching curios run from 19C bronzes and flintlock pistols, to poachers' vintage fishing 'tridents', gamekeepers' mantraps and model ships.

Open daily.

Around Hay Markets

Held every Thursday throughout the year, come rain or shine, Hay's **Thursday Market** goes back 700 years. Once upon a time, traders would walk into town leading pack ponies, or on horseback, their panniers chock-a-block with goods for sale. A round trip of 25 miles would not be uncommon and stabling was provided by the town's inns, which at their peak numbered 41.

Livestock sales continued in the streets until 1919, when the present Cattle Market was built, just off Church Street. Sales still take place here every Thursday, though nowadays sheep have replaced cattle.

Today's market focus is the town square, with Hay Castle looming above, and the adjacent ancient buildings of Cheese Market and Butter Market. Stalls also spill down the hill to the Clock Tower. By the standards of yesteryear, today's market is small, numbering around 40 traders, but, packed into a tight picturesque space, it retains much of its age-old bustling and colourful atmosphere.

Trading starts officially at 8am, though some stallholders may set up a little later. Fruit and vegetables, local meat, fish and game, freshly ground coffee, hot homemade takeaways, deli items, cheese and dairy, herbs and spices, preserves and chutneys, artisan bread, homemade cakes, pastries and savouries, all whet the appetite. Non-food items include jewellery, clothing, home wares, African rugs and baskets, handmade soaps and cosmetics, plants, flowers, garden items, bric-a-brac and more.

100% Hay

Joe and Sein's produce arrives at market every Thursday from their organic smallholding on the outskirts of Hay, which trades under the name 100% Hay. Supplementing their field-fresh fruit and veg are homemade kimchi, award-winning curry pastes, and a particularly rich tasty raw-milk cheese made from their own Anglo-Nubian goats. www.100percenthay.com.

Other market traders who are '100% Hay' in everything but their trading name, include: Hay's very own artisan baking deity, **Alex Gooch**, www.alexgoochbaker.com; **Walkers Cottage**, for preserves, honey, apple juice, (plus herb sea salt and Provençal recipe confectionery), www.walkers-cottage.co.uk; **Veg-Out Hay**, for unusual and tasty snacks such as a kimchi & cheese toasted ciabatta or Spring ribollita soup with fresh basil pesto; **Tam's Jams** for preserves; **Kate's Bakery** for bread and cakes.

The Cheese Market

The Cheese Market was built around 1835 on the site of Hay's pre-17C Guildhall. Then, as now, it comprises an upper room supported on pillars, with an open space below, formerly used as a cheese market. The Lord of the Manor's Court once received taxes and fines here from tenant farmers and market traders. The upper room's many later uses included theatre, chapel, Masonic Hall and Catholic Church. It now offers holiday accommodation.

Below, colourful tiles depict iconic local images, including the Welsh mountain pony, the Herefordshire bull, a gavel (as used by the market auctioneer) and so on. Panels also illustrate episodes and regular events in local history, including The Hiring Fairs, when agricultural workers were taken on, and dancing bears came to town, and the tragic tale of hill farmer, Rosa Blanche Williams, who rode 12 miles to Hay Market every week. Returning home on 22 December 1925, she was caught in a blizzard, thrown from her horse and froze to death.

In addition to the Thursday Market, the Cheese Market also hosts the **Friday Vintage Market** *(Mar-Oct)* selling clothing, accessories, collectibles and homewares. **The Saturday Produce Market** *(all year)* offers homemade pastries, cakes and artisan bread. You'll also find Simon and Carole's African rugs and baskets and Annie Fraser's Greenspinner woollens and hand-spun yarns.

The Butter Market

This open colonnaded Doric temple-like hall was built by a local entrepreneur in 1830. It replaced an ancient open market, providing a covered area for the shelter of local traders and farmers on rainy market days. Bright heraldic banners are slung from the roof and affixed to the railings between the columns. It's odd to think that from 1945 until 1985, when it was re-opened and restored, it had been walled up and used as an egg packing station.

In addition to the Thursday Market, the Butter Market also hosts the **Friday and Saturday Flea Market** *(except Jan)* featuring an eclectic range of bric-a-brac, antiques, collectables, jewellery, books and vintage items.

NOTICE.

Pursuant to the Licensing
Act, 1953, intoxicating Liquors ar
permitted to be sold and supplied i
these Premises between the hours c
10a.m. and 11a.m. and 3p.m and
5p.m. on Mondays and Thursdays
except Christmas Day, for the
accommodation of persons attending
the Marts and Markets

Around the Butter Market

Hay has several shops dealing in antique and vintage goods but if you want it all under one roof, **Hay Antique Market** offers a choice of over 20 dealers, selling an eclectic mix of antiques and collectables at all price ranges. *Homes and Antiques* magazine recently chose it as one of the top 70 places to buy antiques in Britain. *www.hayantiquemarket.co.uk. Open daily.*

Next door in a lovely old half-timbered property is **Clock Tower Books** where you can browse a broad range of books from around 20 dealers. *Open daily.*

Moving along, in an equally ancient building, **Charlotte of Hay** sells funky (new) clothing, crystals, jewellery and accessories, incense, aromatherapy supplies and other hippy-inspired paraphernalia. Everything sold here is either Fairtrade or otherwise ethically sourced. *www.charlottes-of-hay.co.uk. Open daily.*

On the opposite side of the Butter Market, **Bain and Murrin** is a shrine to vintage shopping, fronted by Hay's 'Lady Junk', the ebullient Becky Bain, 'purveyor of best quality tat'. It's all good tongue-in-cheek fun, as you might guess from the kitschy, ever-changing attention-grabbing window displays. The ground floor (*pic below*) is largely clothing including Becky's own beaded and embroidered brooches and bracelets, while downstairs is a softly-lit Aladdin's Cave of furniture and household goods. *Open daily.*

Two doors down, in a town renowned for its independence, **Pughs at Londis** is proof that even a national brand name can work with the community (all Londis stores are independently owned and have their own stocking policies). Aside from local groceries and bakery goods, this is also the place to buy your 'local currency' – **Hay Vouchers** – the idea of shop owner Debbie Davies. These come in various denominations and can be used as money at any participating business in Hay. Over £22,000-worth are in circulation and 95% of businesses accept them, so they make a perfect present for the Hayophile in your life. *Open daily.*

The Killer from the Atom Factory

From 1947–1949, the building now occupied by Hay Antique Market *(pic above)* was home to Little Atom Electrical Products Ltd ('The Atom Factory'), leased by Brian Donald Hume. Although not evident to the people of Hay, Hume was in fact a violent con man and bootlegger. He moved out of Hay in 1949 to London and that year murdered his crooked business associate, Stanley ('The Spiv') Setty. Hume then dismembered him and dropped the body parts from a private plane into the sea. Unfortunately for Hume, Setty's body floated back into the Essex Marshes and Hume was arrested. However, as the police could not prove he was the killer, he received only 12 years for being an accessory to murder. On his release, Hume was paid by a newspaper to admit to killing Setty, safe in the knowledge that he could not be tried twice for the same murder because of the law of 'double jeopardy' (an 800-year-old legal anomaly, abolished in 2005 for serious offences). Hume subsequently fled to Switzerland under a false identity, where he resumed his life of crime, briefly returning to the UK (it's said he was spotted in Hay) and committing armed robbery in Brentford. Fleeing back to Switzerland he repeated the crime, this time shooting and killing a taxi driver. He was caught by the Swiss Police, and achieved the unique distinction of facing trial twice for two different murders in two different countries. Hume was deported to the UK and incarcerated in Broadmoor in 1976. He was released in 1988 but died a few months later.

There's more shop-front kitsch to goggle next door, where the façade of **Goosey Ganders** features not only golden geese (named Gilbert and George after the Shoreditch artists) but shocking pink flamingos (Chiclet and Concetta – from the John Waters' movie *Female Trouble*). Not the obvious name, nor imagery for a lighting shop selling some very serious chandeliers. Swarovski? *Ja!* Venetian? *Si!* Bohemian? *Ano!* Antique English Osler? Of course! And much more global glass besides. The interior is a glitter-ball cave of stalactites with light bouncing from myriad facets, around which you have to duck and weave to get to the desk of genial shop owner and expert chandelier restorer, Simon Farrell. "Don't worry," he says reassuringly, as I catch a £2,000 Murano Glass Mazega chandelier with my elbow, "I can soon put it back together!" *Open daily.*

If your eyes need a rest after the bright lights, cross opposite (just left) to the calming period pastel shades of **Llewelyn & Co**, one of Hay's most elegant shops *(pic below, right)*. It is owned and managed by the ever-friendly easy-going John and Anna Llewelyn. Anna grew up in a classic Welsh Georgian farmhouse and has brought her heritage to Hay in the shape of furniture and decorative goods for the home. Alongside these are a harmonious mix of high-end antique French and Scandinavian furniture and fittings, all personally sourced by Anna and John. Upstairs are smaller pieces, accessories and children's clothes.

www.llewelynandcompany.com. Closed Sun & Tue.

Return, the other side of the Butter Market, to Hay Antique Market and turn left.

Beer Revolution

You think you know the world of beer? Here, your head will spin, even before a drop touches your lips. Among the myriad of truly weird and wonderful creations stocked here, you can sip a *Stillwater Vacuum Black*, polish off a *Pirate Life Mosaic IPA*, or whet your whistle with a *Wu Gang Chops The Tree* (a foraged herb sourish Hefeweisse that goes very nicely with a curry). And no, we didn't make any of those up.

In addition to a selection of around 200 beers and ciders from all over the world, Beer Revolution also supports dozens of local products. And if you can't wait until you get home to quench your thirst, or sate your curiosity, the good news is that this is not just a shop, but also a bang-on-trend bar, with five taps dispensing a rotating selection of some of the world's tastiest craft beers and ciders. There's a cosy walled garden for warm weather quaffing and a kitchen serving snacks *(see p112)*. Cheers, Prost, Na Zdravi!

www.beerrevolution.co.uk. Open Mon–Thur 10am–5pm, Fri–Sat 10am–10pm, Sun 12pm–5pm.

Coming out of Beer Revolution, turn right towards another hophead's delight, Kilverts Hotel.

Kilverts Hotel

This Hay landmark was formerly Pemberton House, a late Georgian remodelling of a 17C building, but has long been a popular pub *(see p113)* and hotel, named in honour of Reverend Francis Kilvert *(see p101)*, even though it has no tangible connection to the 19C diarist.

To either side of Kilverts are antiques and vintage shops respectively. **Haywain**, a new addition to Hay, are specialists in high-end period furniture, porcelain, silverware, pictures, oriental ware and toys. *www.haywainantiques.uk. Open daily.* By contrast, **Fleur de Lys** is a 35-year old town stalwart, with an eclectic collection of clothes, toys, posters, country-style furniture, clocks and watches and garden odds and ends. Its specialism is railways and transport, selling books, model trains and railway ephemera. *Open daily.*

The Hay Makers Gallery

The genesis of this gallery goes back to 1987, when three of today's Hay Makers were asked by Hay Festival founder, Peter Florence, to produce a one-off exhibition for his fledgling festival at Clyro Court. The exhibition was so well received that the three joined forces with six other like-minded makers, and opened a permanent premises which is today's Gallery. Together they comprise some of the finest contemporary professional designer-makers in Britain, working with wood, pottery, stone, textiles, fine wire and other media. Visiting artists add to the variety.

You can spend as much, or as little as you like; from beautiful one-off pieces, silver jewellery and camel leather boxes made by Tuareg craftsmen from Timbuktu *(see p54)*, to elegant prints, tea towels and greeting cards.

www.haymakers.co.uk; Open daily (closed 1.30–2pm Mon–Sat).

If The Welsh Girl sandwich board is outside, climb the steps by the side of the chapel.

Welsh Tapestry Blankets

These beautiful items were traditionally given as wedding presents and handed down as heirlooms. The traditional Welsh tapestry blanket design is double weave which means it is reversible. In 1926 there were 217 mills spread across every Welsh county, today just eight remain, one of which weaves The Welsh Girl designs *(see p54)*.

The Welsh Girl

'Modern Welsh Heritage' is what's promised here, and we think Julie Leonard's innovative contemporary take on ponchos, scarves, bags, cushions and patchworks, all designed and handmade here, is spot on. Her speciality is pure new wool double-weave reversible ponchos in colours exclusive to The Welsh Girl. Also exclusive is her own design Coler Cwtch ('cosy collar') scarf range; a clever variant on the traditional neckgear. All The Welsh Girl lines are woven on looms that once produced Welsh tapestry blankets. Only small runs of cloth are produced, no two colour combinations are ever repeated, cushions are one-of-a-kind and bags three-of-a-kind. So, the chances of bumping into someone else with the same as you are as slim as finding a Kindle in a Hay shop.

www.thewelshgirl.com. Open Thu–Sat, also bank hols and festivals.

A Town of Books too

In 2007 Hay was twinned with Timbuktu, the mysterious city set on the edge of the Sahara Desert, in present-day Mali. When the twinning was officially announced, the Mayor of Hay commented, "We lie on exactly the same line of longitude (3° W). It was meant to be".

Timbuktu claims to be the home of the written word in Africa, with its Golden Age of learning in the 15th and 16th centuries. The libraries in the city once boasted hundreds of thousands of medieval manuscripts, though it has only been very recently that Western academics have woken up to this fact. Before then, it was widely believed that most African history was passed orally through the generations. The recent occupation by al-Qaida has provided one of the greatest threats to this heritage. Fortunately, despite some theft and destruction, most of the manuscripts have been saved by the courageous actions of Timbuktu's librarians and the many other people in Mali who risked their lives, smuggling these treasures south to the capital Bamako, and to elsewhere not under the yoke of al-Qaida. Read all about it in *The Book Smugglers of Timbuktu* by Charlie English.

For more on Hay's links with Timbuktu and the ways in which Hay is helping its literary twin in distress, visit *www.hay2timbuktu.org*, founded by Anne Brichto (see p57).

St John's Chapel

Founded c1254, the Chapel of St John the Baptist began life as a chantry chapel and chapel for the Guild of Tradesmen. It is said that John Wesley preached here, but this is uncertain, and it may have been elsewhere in Hay (possibly at the Ebenezer Chapel, *see p72*). The building was converted to a gaol in 1810 and was in use until 1875, when it was pronounced too insanitary even for prisoners. In subsequent years it was used as a butcher's, a saddler's and a barber's shop, a school and a fire station. It was rebuilt in 1934. Today, half the building functions as a chapel (*mass 10am every Thu*), the other half houses St John's Place, one of the town's best restaurants (*see p112*).

Tomatitos

Despite taking up the infamous home of The Wheatsheaf Pub in 2012 – closed down after police were called out several times to "incidents of crime and disorder" (a phrase very rarely used these days in Hay!) – Tomatitos is not only one of the town's most popular places for food (*see p114*), it's also well patronised by local drinkers.

It was here that Richard Booth first told the press of his plans for Hay's Independence while meeting a journalist from *The Sunday Mirror*. He recalls the meeting in his autobiography: *"Hay is going Independent of Britain", I said. "Do the people of Hay support you?" he said, nostrils quivering. "Yes", I replied, they're all for it". I had only thought of the idea five minutes before.*

Street by Street: Lion Street

Addyman Books

Hay Cinema Bookshop is bigger, Richard Booth's Bookshop is grander, but to get the full dose of Hay fever you have to visit Addymans. This 'well-loved burrow of books' specialises in English literature, modern first editions and rare and out-of-print books and Penguin paperbacks. Like the Tardis, it belies its outer dimensions, and takes its visitors to different times and places.

The ground floor room, left, features gilded sky-blue panels and part of an altar salvaged from a Transylvanian church. The first floor is a classic 1930s-style book readers' snug, covered floor to ceiling with modern first editions and comfy chairs and sofa. Continue up, past the Steampunk-themed room, past the Bat Cave and the Celtic-Arthurian niche, and you'll find a mezzanine floor-cum-landing devoted to travel and exploration, kitted out in the style of Captain Robert Scott's Antarctic hut. As one journalist put it, "You could get lost all afternoon in this shop".

The owners are Derek Addyman and his wife Anne Brichto. Derek, a Hayite, born a couple of hundred yards from the shop, began learning the trade in his teens in the 1960s, moving books, first physically, then through the tills, for Richard Booth in the Hay Cinema Bookshop (see p80).

"In ten years there I handled three or four million books. Unbelievable. I was in charge of books in foreign tongues. And I couldn't read any of them. We priced them by weight. And by how common or unusual a language is. A book in Mandarin? Common. A book in Hawaiian, that will cost you more".

The first Addyman shop began in a back room of The Blue Boar pub in 1987 but quickly moved to their current premises; since then they have spawned two other outlets, The Addyman Annexe (see p33) and Murder & Mayhem (see p59). There's not a page in the Hay Booktown chapter that Derek has not been on, and his tongue-in-cheek claim to be Prince Regent of Hay is hardly overstated. In 2012 he gained national publicity by campaigning that Kindles and e-readers should be banned from Hay, and there are still 'No Kindles' signs at the Addyman shops. His favourite sale? Patrick Stewart buying a First Edition of *Waiting for Godot* and being so excited he called a friend while in the shop to say: "I can't wait to get it home and read it".

www.hay-on-wyebooks.com. Open daily.

Bookstagram

This is a relatively new trend on Instagram where users share pictures of their favourite books. Anne Brichto, co-owner of Addymans, has embraced the movement, and with her beautifully crafted postings, hosts one of the country's most popular accounts. In 2017, taking the idea one step further, Anne, together with Ruth Holloway of Richard Booth's Bookshop, organised the world's first ever '#bookstagram event' as part of the town's 40th Independence anniversary celebrations. Turning social media into social reality, it brought book lovers to Hay from all over Europe and even North America, for workshops, author talks, films and other events. Repeated in 2018, as part of Hay Independence celebrations, with even more events, Bookstagram looks set to become an important part of the Hay calendar.

Cross the road

The Lion Street Gallery

Hay's premier art gallery showcases artists who work in Wales and the Borders. It was founded by Brent Blair, a talented artist in his own right, who in his early days helped create costumes for *Starlight Express*, transformed people into werewolves with prosthetic makeup and worked as an animatronics creative on *Little Shop of Horrors* at Pinewood Studios.

www.lionstreetgallery.co.uk. Closed Tue & Sun.

Murder & Mayhem

Part of the Addyman triumvirate, Murder & Mayhem, established 1997, is dedicated to things that go bump in the night. It is the town's most specialised and one of its most popular bookshops, with its fiendishly decorated window display and fascinatingly themed interior, intriguing and delighting both dedicated specialists and 'ordinary' passers-by with its eye-goggling appeal. You'll find detective and horror books covering all literary periods plus a true crime section including works on 'Hay Murderers', Donald Hume *(see p49)* and Herbert Rowse Armstrong *(see p70-71)*. Just make sure no-one steps on you – or calls the police – if you decide to lie down for a selfie inside the chalk body outline *(see opposite)*!

www.hay-on-wyebooks.com. Open daily.

Rawhide

Owner Suzy Branson has a fine eye for contemporary design, and her shop, which takes its name from the on-trend animal hides sold here, has some of the most desirable lighting, scarves and throws, leather bags and exclusive-design greeting cards in Hay. Add to that, jewellery and homeware from leading brands in Europe and Scandinavia and, exclusively to Wales, *Moomin* mugs and paraphernalia, all set to broaden its cult popularity in 2019, with a new animated TV series.

Open Mon–Sat.

Eighteen Rabbit

Eighteen Rabbit, in case you didn't know, was the early 8C Mayan Ruler of Copan, set on the border between Guatemala and Honduras. He was also patron of the arts and responsible for a cultural renaissance in his kingdom. In 2005 current shop proprietors, Andrew and Louise, came across his story while travelling through Central America, but were dismayed to see that this once vibrant culture had, over the centuries, been largely lost, and that its products and handicrafts were now effectively in fealty to the rich nations of the First World. They decided that when they got back to Britain they would sell fairly traded arts, crafts and gifts from around the world, with a focus on style and design. Typical of their merchandise is the beautiful 'Hope & Peace' jewellery from Cambodia, made from recycled bullets and bomb shell casings. "These were one of the first lines we sourced when we opened the shop in 2012," says Andrew, "turning swords into plough-shares…"

If confirmation were needed, *Condé Nast Traveller* recently called Eighteen Rabbit "the coolest Fair Trade outlet ever". Kids love the colourful flip flop animals, bearded trendies flip through lifestyle magazines, and everyone adores their clothing and accessories.

By the way, Eighteen Rabbit's real name was Uaxaclajuun Ub'aah K'awiil, but even the most creative people of Hay-on-Wye would struggle with that as a brand name.

www.eighteenrabbit.co.uk. Open daily.

Cross the road.

Hay Deli

You just know that Hay Deli is going to be healthy and tasty – not to mention stylish and trendy – by its exterior and window display, and inside it doesn't disappoint. This is the town's go-to for the very best in local and organic produce, delicatessen goods, and wholefoods: bread by Alex Gooch, cheese by Neal's Yard Creamery (from nearby Dorstone) and organic skincare products by Herbfarmacy (from nearby Eardisley), to name but three. Elsewhere the shelves are packed with a cornucopia of specialist foods.

Hay Deli also stocks a very good range of local drinks and vintage wines. Speaking of which, the building was formerly a hall of the Rechabite movement, a 19C Friendly Society, part of the British temperance movement. Ironically, it was later converted to become the Red Lion.

www.haydeli.co.uk. Open daily.

The Table

This intimate contemporary art gallery, which has something of the domestic charm of a mini Kettles Yard (Cambridge), boasts an eclectic stable of local artists. With an emphasis on drawing, the work ranges from large oil paintings through to more abstracted pieces. On Sunday lunchtimes you can enjoy the authentic Italian taste of Nonna Caterina's pasta.

www.thetablehay.com. Open Thu–Sat (during exhibitions) and every Sun lunchtime (www.nonnacaterina.co.uk).

RUD- WILLIAMS
& SONS LTD
HAY
DEPARTMENTS
HIGH TOWN
FURNISHING & BUILDERS
IRONMONGERY
LION ST
AGRICULTURAL IMPLEMENTS
& DAIRY GOODS.
FURNITURE, BED HEADS.
BEDDING & LINOLEUMS.
CHINA, GLASS & EARTHENWARE
STATION YARD
COAL, COKE & LIME
BRICKS, PIPES & SLATES
SAW MILLS
ENGLISH & FOREIGN TIMBER

RICHARD BOOTH
ht Anywhere in the

Secondhand
and
New Bo

CAFE

Secondhand
and
New Books

Richard Booth's Bookshop

This is the Harrods of the Hay bookshop world, and a place of pilgrimage that no bibliophile should miss, as much for its history as its gorgeous interior, and of course its books, both second-hand and new. And once you've had enough book shopping for the day, there's an 'ace caff' and bijou cinema in which to relax.

The building dates from 1886, when it was an agricultural warehouse/showroom called The Limited. It was the first business in town to be a limited liability concern, hence its rather prosaic name; original tiles remain on the front of the shop and the original sign (The Limited) remains on the frontage next door, now a separate shop. Another vestige of this era is the Robert William & Sons sign on a stairwell.

Richard Booth *(see p13)* purchased the premises in 1963, its cavernous three-level interior ideal for accommodating his book-buying bonanzas. It soon filled to overflowing with volumes from all over the globe and became the world's largest second-hand bookshop (these days it still claims to be the largest in Europe).

However, by 2007, when Booth's was sold to American businesswoman Elizabeth Haycox, the roof leaked, the heating didn't work and a general state of chaos reigned. Indeed, one of Booth's staff recalls him saying, *"We've got to remake this building, we've got a mess and it's my fault, I am an anarchist".* A Guardian journalist concurred, *"Gloriously unkempt... every subject can be found in the dark recesses of his utterly misnamed The Limited".*

Little by little, Haycox's new broom swept clean, dismaying some die-hard Boothophiles, but delighting the majority of the book-buying public. She invested a small fortune in repairs and renovations, restored floorboards to their present gleam, increased natural light into the shop, added toilets and a lift, comfy old sofas and armchairs, pot plants and art works. Most scandalously, as far as the old regime was concerned, she also added new books to supplement the core collection of second-hand volumes. Today the shelves bear the weight of half a million books, managed by specialist department heads; another significant departure from the old days, when knowledgeable staff were hard to find.

The building's changes have not just been about books. The lower floor is home to a light airy chic **café** *(see p116)*; to the side (separate entrance) is a cosy little 47-seat **cinema** with exposed rubble walls and mezzanine seating area; on the third floor is a studio used for yoga and pilates. **Hay Music** concerts, featuring Baroque, Classical and Contemporary Chamber music, are also regularly held in the main bookshop *(www.haymusic.org)*.

www.boothbooks.co.uk. Open daily.

Bartrums

If Booth's, or indeed anywhere in Hay has stimulated you to pick up pen and paper, then Bartrums is the place to start. Behind its Dickensian bow-window frontage are two floors of 'fine writing tools' from all over the world, the very finest of these luxuriously displayed in Edwardian cabinets. Look out too for elegant French leather goods, stylish Italian journals, all kinds of stationery, handmade books, plus a wide range of *Tin Tin* merchandise.

www.bartrums.co.uk. Open daily.

Continue down Lion Street.

The Poetry Bookshop

In 2016 more than a million poetry books were sold in Britain, the highest number on record. So perhaps it was no surprise when The Poetry Bookshop, which offers the most comprehensive collection of poetry for sale in the UK, moved to more prominent, handsome new premises in the town in 2017. The old shop was co-founded in the mid-1970s by Anne Stevenson, a poet and Sylvia Plath, biographer. The new shop stocks some 10,000 rare, out-of-print, new and used poetry books, from fine period bindings and First Editions to cheaper paperbacks; from John Keats and Gerard Manley Hopkins to contemporary wordsmiths, Carol Ann Duffy and Kate Tempest.

Current owners, Chris and Melanie Prince, who have been Hay's poetry custodians for nearly 20 years, say that their new large, light, airy shop, now in a prominent town position, is very much a statement about bringing poetry to the forefront in Hay. Its open aspect and cool grey-and-charcoal colour scheme echoes the best of modern High Street design, and reflects the pared down, uncluttered aesthetic of poetry.

Ticket sales for The Poetry Bookshop Relaunch Party, starring celebrated punk-poet Dr John Cooper Clarke, broke box office records at The Globe *(see p72)* that evening.

www.poetrybookshop.com. Open Mon–Sat.

*Look left, up the short pedestrianised street known as The Pavement. At the junction with Lion Street, the small unit below the corner property was once The Bear Pit where dancing bears were kept when The Hiring Fairs (see p46) came to town. Continuing down Lion Street, the two ornately gabled houses next to The Poetry Bookshop date from the 17C and 18C; both now house antiques shops. **The Sitting Room Gallery** stocks some beautiful antique carpets and rugs, while **Hazy Days** specialises in retro pieces (both usually open weekends only).*

Golesworthys

The Golesworthy family have been on this site since 1877, when Frank Woodland Golesworthy set up his outfitters, making this the longest established family-run concern in Hay. The building itself dates from the early 1800s. Don't be misled by its somewhat old-fashioned frontage; step in, and alongside traditional classic tweeds, Barbours and iconic Stetson headwear, are the latest outdoor clothing ranges from the likes of Berghaus, Seeland, Härkila, Caterpillar, Helly Hansen, and other premium trending brands. This is also an excellent place for walkers to stock up on maps, bags and general kit. *www.golesworthys.com. Open daily.*

The Clock Tower

Completed in 1884 at a cost of £600, the clock tower was part of a much grander Victorian building scheme that included a public hall and corn exchange. Due to a lack of funds, however, these were never built.

The Granary

This popular café, set in a sympathetically restored agricultural warehouse on two floors, has been refreshing Hay since 1979 *(see p114)*. On a warm afternoon its sunny terrace is perfect for watching the world go by.

Cross the road diagonally left.

Rose's Bookshop

Prepare to go misty eyed with nostalgia in Rose's, which will take you back not only through your own childhood, but through many generations before yours. Rose's have been here since 1995 and deal only in rare and out-of-print collectable children's books including *Biggles* and *Rupert Bear*, and annuals from the *Dandy*, *Beano*, *Eagle* and many more. Evergreen authors such as Roald Dahl, AA Milne, Richmal Crompton, Michael Morpurgo and Jacqueline Wilson rub dust jackets with unexpected names such as Dylan Thomas and David Walliams. More valuable volumes range from a First Edition of *The Tale of Peter Rabbit* to a signed First Edition of *Words & Pictures* by Quentin Blake. It's not just UK reading; Rose's has a good stock of American favourites, from works by Dr Seuss and L M Montgomery (*Anne of Green Gables*) to obscurities such as *The Twelve Labors of Wimpole Stout* by Wheaton Phillips Webb. Come here on a rainy day outing with little ones; it's also the perfect place for that special first birthday or christening present.

www.stellabooks.com. Open daily.

Continue on from Rose's to browse the adjacent TARDIS book passage (see pic. p4) – which also gives a view into the lovely garden of Tinto House, one of Hay's best B&Bs. Continue down Broad Street.

The Old Electric Shop

This handsome old property, formerly occupied by Y Gelli (Hay) Council Chambers – look high on the building for the name – was rechristened when Hannah Burson arrived here in 2012. The Old Electric Shop was the name of her previous premises on Castle Street, formerly belonging to South Wales Electricity, and there's no doubt Hannah bought a buzz along with the name; "I can't resist pieces with an industrial or commercial history", she says. But there's a lot more here, besides chic shop fittings and funky factory furniture. Older pieces, such as vintage kitchenettes, and fairground and circus memorabilia, sit comfortably with carefully chosen new pieces, such as artisan workwear, creative upholstery, jaunty trilbies, bang-on-trend letterpress prints and cards, books with titles like *The Art of Whittling*, and maybe a jellyfish encased in a glass cube.

The Old Electric Shop is also a good pit stop for a coffee and cake or lunch (*see p115*). Look on the blackboard for evening events (usually Thursdays) which might include live music/comedy, speed chess, poker, drawing, book appreciation... During festivals, cocktails and live music are served up nightly. At any time of the year, it's where the local, and non-local 'Hay-listers' hang out; Robert Plant, David Hasselhoff, Will Young, Chris Evans and Tony Robinson have all been spotted here.

www.oldelectric.co.uk. Open daily.

Next door to the Rose & Crown is Williams & Beales, which has been a solicitors' office for over a century. In 1906 Herbert Rowse Armstrong (see pp70–71) started work here as a clerk. Next door but one, the unusually decorated building, now home to the fish ' n' chips shop, used to be the post office.

Broad Street Book Centre

This fine old early-17C black-and-white building houses around 20 individual book sellers, most with their own little nook, complete with seat, where you can disappear into a good book for as long as you wish. You'll find many subjects here, from angling to Buddhism, sci-fi to theology, railways and military to motorsport, plus Modern First Editions and antiquarian books on all subjects. Hancock & Monks are renowned for their classical music section, including CDs, while Logaston Books represents local interest. The bicycle wheel sign above the shop, *Rest for the Tyred*, refers to the B&B upstairs. *Open Mon–Sat.*

Go past the Black Swan, formerly a pub, now a holiday cottage, and cross the road.

The Three Tuns

Currently awaiting new owners, The Three Tuns, built c1600, is said to be the second oldest secular building in Hay, after the castle. From the 1960s until 2005, when it was ravaged by fire, this was *the* place to be in Hay. Its legendary owner, the redoubtable Lucy Powell, kept it so bloody-mindedly old-fashioned that in 1982 it effortlessly doubled as an early-20C basic country cottage in a film scene of *On the Black Hill* by Bruce Chatwin *(see below)*. In the 1960s it attracted celebrities including Marianne Faithfull, and villains such as The Great Train Robbers, who in 1963 had a drink here while hiding out nearby. More recent celebrity tipplers include Jools Holland, Neil Kinnock and Huw Edwards.

On the Black Hill

This tale of almost unremitting hardship in the Marches won much critical acclaim as a realistic portrayal of early 20C hill farming life in this area. It was written in 1982 by novelist and travel writer, Bruce Chatwin, and is set just south of Hay ('Rhulen' in the novel). The nearest village, Craswall, lies at the foot of the Black Hill, which is known locally as The Cat's Back, popular with walkers. Chatwin first came to the area as a schoolboy in the 1950s, and returned regularly for the rest of his life. Both the book and its 1987 film version won awards.

The Hay Poisoner

The case of Major Herbert Rowse Armstrong has excited attention for nearly a century. Its popularity is easy to understand in that it bears so many familiar themes and stereotypes, though the actual case is much less easy to understand as the telling of the tale varies wildly depending on the narrator.

Version A. The husband, Herbert: retired army officer, mason, church reader, solicitor, nimble dancer, dapper with meticulously waxed moustache, and a womaniser, despite being only 5ft 6in tall and a weedy seven stones. The wife, Katherine: highly strung, a hypochondriac, prone to bouts of sickness, domineering and abusive.

Version B. The husband: most of the above *but* (importantly) a devoted family man with no evidence of womanising. The wife: highly strung? Yes. A hypochondriac? Certainly. And also prone to depression. But demonstrably cared for by her husband and staff.

In 1919 Mrs Armstrong fell ill with nerve damage. By the following year, her already fragile mental state had deteriorated, and she was admitted to an asylum. Some months later she was allowed to return home, but became increasingly depressed. In mid-February she fell violently ill, and within a few days she was dead.

Fast forward eight months, to the Major inviting rival solicitor, Oswald Martin, to tea at his house in Cusop Dingle (a short walk from Hay), supposedly in an effort to reconcile business differences. Some say that with Martin out of the way, Armstrong stood to gain a lot of money. Others dispute that claim. Martin was later to tell the police that Armstrong offered him a cake, with a genteel, "excuse fingers!" Martin subsequently fell sick, showing the same peculiar symptoms as the dying Katherine. The local pharmacist, Fred Davies, who was also not only Oswald Martin's father-in-law, but also bore an old grudge against the Major, made his suspicions clear to Dr Hinks, who had treated Katherine. The doctor would have none of it, but the case took an even more curious turn when a few days later, Martin produced a box of chocolates that had been sent anonymously in the post. Remarkably, Martin and his wife claimed to have eaten a couple of the chocolates, as a result of which his wife had fallen sick. Pressured by Davies, Dr Hinks took a urine sample from Martin and submitted it, along with the chocolates, to the Home Office in London. When traces of arsenic were found in both the urine sample and the chocolates, it was referred to the local police. They duly searched Armstrong's house, found quantities of arsenic, and arrested him.

The Major claimed (not unreasonably, for the time), that he had been using it as a weed killer to keep down his dandelions. Katherine was consequently exhumed and found to have large quantities of the poison inside her. The Major was tried, found guilty and hanged in Gloucester Gaol in 1922. He thus became the first, and only, solicitor in the UK to go to the gallows.

An open and shut case? Not so, according to Martin Beales, also a solicitor, who not only worked in the Major's office in Hay, but remarkably, also lived (until quite recently) in the Armstrongs' old house in Cusop. Beales believed that the Major was innocent, and in 1995 published *Dead not Buried* which argued the case for the defence; it was republished in 1997 under the racier title of *The Hay Poisoner*. Beales suggests that, in the best Agatha Christie tradition, many parties with vested interests in Hay bore not only grudges, but malice against Armstrong, and that they colluded, to a lesser or greater extent, in his being found guilty. But would the Major *really* have sent a box of poisoned chocolates in the post to Martin? At the very least, Beales argues, the prosecution's evidence was purely circumstantial, and in a modern court would have been summarily dismissed.

The story has figured in various other media adaptations since 1952, most recently in 1994 as a BAFTA-winning TV mini-series, *Dandelion Dead*, filmed in Hay, by Mike Hodges. Prior to *Dandelion Dead*, Martin Beales had agreed with the request of Major Armstrong's daughter, Margaret, not to publish his book until after her death. However, after seeing Hodges' series, she was so incensed about how biased it was, that she rang up Beales and told him to publish immediately. You can buy books on the case at Murder and Mayhem (see p59) and you can also learn more by joining Hay Tours' *Armstrong Murder Tours. www.haytours.org.*

We'll let another Cusop Dingle resident, Richard Booth, have the last, and as often is the case, irreverent word on the subject, "Hay-on-Wye, the centre of British civilisation, the last place to hang a solicitor".

Cross the road and turn left

The Globe

Housed in the Ebenezer Chapel, built in 1845, The Globe has been the town's arts and entertainment centre since 2000. It is usually open five nights a week, hosting an eclectic mix of music and arts events, including folk, acoustic and world music, DJs, occasional theatre, poetry, spoken word, philosophy and Desert Island Picks with a local personality as the 'castaway'. The Globe is also the beating heart of the HowTheLightGetsIn Festival *(see p75).*

Many events are free, most cost no more than £5 (in advance) and are terrific value. The Globe is also often open during the day, when you can enjoy a coffee and its rotating art/photography exhibitions. Downstairs is The Globe at Hay Kitchen *(see p111).*

Regular free events include: the ever popular Tuesday Open Mic Night, showcasing the town's profuse musical talent; the quirky Death Café, tackling the complex ideas that surround death (second Tuesday of the month); Philosophy Café (every other Thursday); Quiz Night (first Friday of the month) and Lego Club for kids (every Sunday). For details of all regular events *see p121.*

www.globeathay.org.

The street beside the Globe, Heol Y Dwr (meaning Water Street), was once a leet taken off the Dulas Brook, which runs down into what was the industrialised part of Hay, just below here by the river *(see p86).* There, the rushing water would power fulling mills, dedicated to clothes-making, before emptying into the Wye.

Go up Heol Y Dwr and turn right into Brook Street. Just before the Pottery, look left up Chancery Lane. In spring and summer this pretty terrace is festooned with brightly coloured hanging baskets.

Brook Street Pottery and Gallery

This colourful gallery displays works by some of the best contemporary studio potters in Britain. It focuses mainly on the functional but there are also some lovely ornamental pieces, including jewellery and sculptural work with items for all budgets. At the back of the shop, the engaging owner, Simon Hulbert, has his studio where he makes highly individual frost-proof garden vessels (including some oversize 'showstoppers') all moulded from the special blend of terracotta that Simon prepares with added stoneware for strength. Pieces by international potters and sculptors who have worked with Simon in Hay are also on show.

If your budget doesn't run to one-of-a kind pieces, fret not, the shop's standard range of hand-thrown plant pots are produced to the same high-fired standard and will still grace your garden. Regular changing exhibitions are staged in the light-filled timber-framed area upstairs.

Open Wed–Sat.

Continue up Brook Street, past Richard Booth's Bookshop Cinema and you are back in the heart of town on Lion Street.

Big Ideas and a 'Crack-in' Festival

The Globe at Hay is an offshoot of the Institute of Arts and Ideas (based in London), founded in 2008 by one of the country's leading philosophers, Hilary Lawson, "with the aim of returning philosophy to big ideas and putting them at the centre of culture... an urgent call to rethink where we are". In turn, this has spawned the HowTheLightGetsIn Festival, which takes its name from a Leonard Cohen lyric (*there is a crack in everything...that's how the light gets in*). It is the largest philosophy gathering of its kind in the world, where philosophers, scientists, politicians, journalist, writers and other prominent national and local personalities debate topical burning issues. However, you don't have to get your kicks from Wittgenstein's *Tractatus* to attend. HTLGI is not just about 'big ideas'; it includes comedy, music, documentary films, poetry, banquets, a masked ball, fairground rides and a Spiegel Circus, all set in some of the most exotic tents and marquees this side of Morocco. No need to worry about muddy feet here.

Past speakers and artists have included Rowan Williams, Diane Abbott, Polly Toynbee, AS Byatt, Martin Amis, Michael Howard, Angela Eagle, and on the musical and comedy fronts, Laura Marling, Fairport Convention, British Sea Power, Marcus Brigstocke and Robin Ince. By the standards of Hay Festival it might be classified as small talk, but in 2016 (2017 was a fallow year) it attracted an audience of nearly 40,000, which in any other terms is very respectable.

Frustratingly, or conveniently, depending on your viewpoint, most years HTLGI has clashed or coincided with the Hay Festival. There is no connection between the two, nor any love lost between them. Attendees of both say they enjoy the friendly intimate scale of HTLGI and the fact that it is mostly free of corporate interests. Local shops are also pleased to have a festival in the centre of town. In past years, HTLGI was staged for the same 11-day duration as the Hay Festival of Literature. In 2018, however, it focused on the first four days of the late May bank holiday weekend, cramming in 400 events, 150 debates and talks, featuring 150 bands and 500 artists, spread over 12 stages.

www.hay.htlgi.iai.tv.

Hay! Did You Know That...

It is the humble Dulas Brook, and not the mighty River Wye, which forms the border between England and Wales, dividing Welsh Hay and English Cusop.

Hay only became Hay-on-Wye in 1955, reputedly after the local postmaster became fed up of receiving mail (mis)addressed to Hoy, in the Orkneys. However, only people "from off" ever use its full name, to locals it's always (just) Hay.

Britain's longest ancient monument, Offa's Dyke, passes right through the centre of Hay, though you'd never know it. The actual dyke has long gone but the Offa's Dyke Path marks its way.

Hay Festival may not be the oldest literary festival in Britain – that title goes to Cheltenham, founded 1949 – but it is the biggest (and the best!).

To celebrate Hay Festival's legacy, in 2017 it donated its 30-year media archive to the British Library, in what is said to be the largest single donation of literary recordings in the library's history.

In the early days of the Hay Festival, one of the main venues was the primary school. Journalist Carolyn Hitt: "Time was when the green room was the staff room of the local primary. Salman Rushdie could be found discussing his latest oeuvre under the potato prints of Year Five while the press office consisted of a single fax machine".

The last place in the country where fairies were documented (*The Folklore and Witchcraft of Herefordshire*, 1912, by Ella Mary Leather) is Cusop Dingle, immediately across the Dulas Brook from Hay.

Hay is 'officially' twinned with Timbuktu (Mali), Redu (Belgium), and, according to Hay Festival co-founder, Peter Florence – with tongue firmly in cheek – Ambridge, Hogsmeade and Macondo; the latter being from *One Hundred Years of Solitude* by Gabriel García Márquez. The twinning with Redu has lapsed in recent years due to inactivity, leaving just Timbuktu. Ironically, or perhaps appropriately, this is a place that one third of Britons, polled in a 2006 survey, thought was also fictional.

The second 'official language' of Hay is Gujarati – declared by King Richard (Booth) on the first anniversary of Independence Day in 1978, in honour of Gujarati-speaking guests who came along to the celebrations.

In his heyday, Richard Booth bought so many libraries for cherry-picking that Hay was chock-a-block with unsellable books. A *Daily Telegraph* journalist recalls a book seller showing him 10,000 copies alone of *HM Ploughing Regulations for Bengal* (1948). Many books were simply burned.

Hay not only declared itself independent of the UK in 1977, the following year (also on 1 April) it also declared that it had left the European Union (or European Economic Community as it was then known) – nearly 40 years before the rest of the UK voted likewise. In 2014, when Hay voted to reaffirm that it wished to 'stay independent', there was a turnout of 530, with a resounding 483 'ayes'.

Hay was the first town in Wales, and only the third town in Europe, to ban plastic bags. The plastic-like bags offered by traders in Hay today are made of 100% compostable cornstarch.

The 'Official National Anthem' of Hay is the *Colonel Bogey March*, popularised in *The Bridge On The River Kwai*, and no doubt chosen (by Richard Booth) because of the similarity of Kwai to Wye.

A Walk Along the Wye

On this lovely riverside walk to Hay's very own beach, you'll see a golden postbox, the site of an ancient castle, the routes of long gone trams and trains, and perhaps a rabbit hole or two. There's a perfect spot for a tea party, all that's missing is a Mad Hatter! On a sunny day pack a picnic and maybe even swimming gear. The walk is enjoyable year-round, but in winter can be muddy in parts.

Start at the golden postbox on Church Street, almost opposite Hay Cinema Bookshop.

Hay's Indefatigable Golden Girl

The town's gold pillar box celebrates local hero Josie Pearson. Born in Bristol in 1986, Josie grew up in Cusop, before moving to Hay. A talented show jumper, she was tragically involved in a head-on car collision in 2003. Her 19-year-old boyfriend was killed and she suffered permanent spinal damage resulting in paralysis from the chest down, though retaining use of her shoulders and arms. Determined to continue her sporting ambitions, she met, by chance, a fellow patient at the spinal unit where she was rehabilitating, who was a GB wheelchair rugby player. It sparked her interest in this near-exclusive male sport and, in November 2006, less than a year after taking up wheelchair rugby, she was selected first for the GB squad, then for the 2008 Paralympics team in Beijing. Josie thus became the first woman to compete in wheelchair rugby for GB at this level. Moreover, at just 22, she was not only the sole female, but also the 'baby' on the team.

Despite this milestone, after Beijing, Josie chose to focus on sprinting, which she had tried previously while also playing wheelchair rugby. She was selected to compete in the 2011 World Championships in New Zealand, but despite being expected to medal in four events, she came home empty handed. Disappointed, Josie chose to switch disciplines once again, and went on to qualify for the London Paralympics in both discus and club throw. On 7th September 2012 she finally struck gold with a world record throw of 6.8 metres in the discus, a title which she defended the following year, at the World Championships in Lyon, with another world record throw. In the 2013 New Year Honours, she was awarded the MBE for services to athletics.

Cross the road.

Hay Cinema Bookshop

Only in Hay would a redundant cinema be turned into a bookshop, and still thrive. For a start you'd need enough books to fill it, but in 1965, Richard Booth, who bought the building, had way more than enough! In fact the shop gained an entry in the *Guinness Book of Records*, albeit for only one year, as 'the largest second-hand bookshop in the world', holding 250,000 volumes. Stroll in today and you'll still find around 200,000 books on the shelves, all neatly categorised.

The funny thing is, some people who shop here are not interested in the books' contents. The Cinema Bookshop offers "a huge range of 19C bindings including baskerville, classic, leather and cloth... from as little as £4 per volume". So, if you want to 'pimp' your own library this is the place. And you'd be in good company; Saatchi, Versace and international menswear retailer, Hacketts, are among the many clients who do indeed judge a book solely by its cover.

Bindings aside, much of the 'serious stuff' is upstairs, in the section of around 3,000 volumes managed by Francis Edwards. Established in 1855 in London, they are affiliated to Quinto Bookshop of Charing Cross Road and specialise in travel, natural history, art, architecture, history, naval, military, literature and the social sciences.

From the outside it's not difficult to envisage the building's original function. Inside, it's not so easy, though its surviving starry ceiling is a reminder of those innocent days when Saturday night at the movies was the highlight of the week. In front of the shop are 'honesty crates' of books at £1 each and a curious, slowly oxidising pyramid, partly illuminated by night, once a lover's tryst.

www.haycinemabookshop.co.uk. Open daily.

Cross back over the road.

The Swan Hotel

Somewhat surprisingly, given the town's visitor numbers, The Swan is the only bona fide hotel in Hay. A coaching inn since the 18C, it was rebuilt in its present form c1812. It was completely renovated in 2016 and, under vibrant new ownership, is turning what was a failing Hay institution into a first-class venue for eating and drinking (both formally and informally, *see p112*), meeting and sleeping. On a warm day, its pretty, lawned garden is a lovely spot for a nice cuppa, or something stronger.

Head down Swan Bank (on the corner of The Swan and Church Street).

The Old Castle

Aside from the remains of the motte (mound) there's nothing left of Hay's very first castle. In fact this 'castle' was probably little more than a small fortified timber stockade. A bailey (protective ditch) would once have surrounded it. Climb to the top of the motte and, as you can see, even today, it would have given a very good view of approaching danger. Some sources claim it was built by the Norman Duke, William FitzOsbern, in 1070. A relative and close counsellor of William the Conqueror, he is also known to have fought at the Battle of Hastings. Others say it was built by William Revel, a follower of Hay's very first Lord, Bernard de Neufmarché. Whatever, it didn't remain for long as the town's main castle *(see p34)*.

Just behind here (to the right) is the livestock market, also accessible by a passageway next to Jones Hardware on Castle Street, where, these days, sheep are sold every Thursday morning. Continue down Swan Bank to the church.

St Mary's Church

The site of the Anglo-Catholic parish church goes back to the 12C, which may explain why it was built outside the old town walls, which did not appear until the early 13C. The old church collapsed in the 18C and today's structure dates mostly from the late 19C. Step inside the light spacious interior and to your left, on the opposite wall is a 14C effigy. Local lore says it is the legendary 'giantess' and 'castle builder' Maud de St Valery (aka Moll Walbee), wife of William de Braose (*see p9*). More informed sources say it is from a tomb of one of the early vicars of Hay, or a monk from Brecknock Priory.

The splendid **Bevington Organ**, one of the finest in Wales, is put to excellent regular use by Father Richard Williams (*pic below, also see opp*). In fact St Mary's Church is, alongside The Globe, the town's most prolific music venue. **Hay Music** concerts, featuring Baroque, Classical and Contemporary Chamber music, are regularly held here (as well as at Richard Booth's Boookshop, *www.haymusic.org*), with a three-day festival around late April. St Mary's is also an annual Hay Festival concert venue and has welcomed many special guests, none more so than in 2009 when the Archbishop of Canterbury, Rowan Williams, brought Desmond Tutu along to the church.

From April through September, **Hay Jazz** is a series of monthly cabaret evenings featuring top class jazz musicians such as Alan Barnes (*below*).

www.stmaryschurchhayonwye.co.uk ('Events' for concerts).

A Vampire and a Hunchback in the Church!

Father Richard Williams, incumbent at St Mary's since 2001, is not only the most popular clergyman in Hay for decades, he is also a concert pianist, a gifted organist and composer who has been playing keyboards since he was five years old (the same age he says he knew he was going to become a priest!). In 2015, as part of Hay Festival, Father Richard delighted audiences with his live organ accompaniment to the silent back-and-white film classic, *Nosferatu*. There are many clerics for whom the very idea of a vampire movie inside a church would be anathema. Not the unconventional Father Richard: "I feel sorry for him (Nosferatu), OK, he killed a few people, but..." At the 2016 Festival, Father Richard accompanied another silent classic, *The Hunchback of Notre Dame*, starring Lon Chaney. Such events are also staged throughout the year – just look at the website (opposite). You'll also find Father Richard, most evenings, playing the organ at the church.

Leave St Mary's the way you came in, and turn left, down the adjacent alleyway. On the right, through the railings, you can spy a gorge and the Login Brook. When the path forks, keep left to pass under an old railway tunnel to reach the riverside path. Head left, passing Warren Cottage; note the jokey toilet bowls outside (not for use!). The track you're now on was once the line for Hay's horse-drawn tramway (see p85).

After a few yards you will come to a gate entering The Warren. Go right at the fork, following the track downhill, to a path by the river.

The Warren

This beautiful meadow on the River Wye takes its name from the fact that rabbits were supposedly once bred here, though it's more likely that they just thrived here. For centuries it has been a favourite locals' spot, and on sunny summer days you'll see walkers and families with young children paddling and swimming in the shallow crystal-clear water off the pebbly river beach. Canoeists paddle past regularly, negotiating the mini rapids, adding to the colourful scene. Kingfishers and otters have been seen within the vicinity and the area has been designated an area of Special Scientific Interest (SSI).

In the early 1970s a scheme was proposed to convert this area into a caravan park. Local businessmen and residents, horrified at the prospect of the community losing this beautiful area, decided to club together to purchase the field so that it could continue its existence unchanged. To help fund the upkeep of the Warren, a 200-membership club was set up (now 300 strong), which continues to run today.

There is good fishing on this stretch of the Wye *(see p99)*, though you must have a licence.

www.haywarren.org.uk.

Of Trams and Trains

In the early 19C, road and river links to Hay were so unreliable that a horse drawn-tramway – one of the first in the country – was built, running from South Wales, via Brecon to Hay then Kington. Coal and 'luxury goods' were unloaded off barges from the Brecon & Monmouth Canal and sent to Hay and points north, while lime, corn and other country produce travelled the other way. Construction was completed from Brecon to Hay in 1816, and extended to Eardisley by 1818.

In 1864 the tram was replaced by the Hereford, Hay & Brecon Railway, which offered easier transport but unfortunately had a detrimental effect on the local economy. Plentiful manufactured goods from the cities forced the closure of several small family businesses in Hay, cheap leather goods meant the local tannery was no longer viable and allied trades (such as saddle-making) declined. Commercial flour production and beer-brewing in Hay also ended c1900. The train line eventually closed in the early 1960s. To learn more, take a Historic Railway Tour with Hay Tours.

www.haytours.org.

From the riverside take the track uphill to a parking area. Go through here to the lane ahead. Continue on, ignoring the first fingerpost, and follow the potholed track until it bends left and then immediately right, to pass between the stone embankments of an old railway bridge. Immediately after this, turn left through the gate to join a path that was once the railway line. After a short while it becomes broader and the cuttings to either side give a better sense of it once being a railway line. Once you reach the stone benches on the right, you are back at the point at which you passed under the old railway line earlier in the walk. From this point on, there was only ever one track, originally built for the tramway, subsequently used by the railway. Just below is a lower path, but keep on this upper track which continues to the road bridge. There are fine views up and down the river from the top of the bridge, so you might like to make a quick detour, up the steps, at this point.

Hay Bridge

The current bridge over the River Wye, dating from 1957, is the fourth. The first was built in 1763, before that the only crossing was by ford, or by ferry; a dangerous, sometimes fatal undertaking when the river was in spate.

Immediately after the bridge, take the left-hand fork. Follow this into the car park. Continue straight ahead through the car park, through a gate beside the sewage pumping station where the track disappears into grass. This is where the Dulas Brook pours into the River Wye and is as far as you can go. Look right and you can see where the bridge, long gone, once carried the railway line. Return to the car park and turn left beside the house called Chantic into Wyeford Road.

At the junction with the main road, the blue plaque, high on the wall of Lamb House, marks the old Nyport Gate. On the other side of the road, almost opposite, is another blue plaque that commemorates Hay Town Well, used in medieval times.

Cross the road and take the short flight of steps by the plaque, up to a narrow path, signposted Wye Valley Walk and Black Lion Green. You are now following the line of the old town walls. Beware brambles to your right, but here, as you stand in Wales, enjoy the open views to the left over English fields and down to the large Hay & Brecon Farmers warehouse on the main road. This is the site of Hay Railway Station, closed in 1961. After a couple of minutes or so, pass through a gate, go past four houses, then take a sharp left down the steep slope.

Black Lion Green

This pretty greensward by the Dulas Brook has a dark past. In 1742 an itinerant Calvinist preacher named William Seward came here to address a large crowd. Seward had a hardline reputation that had annoyed his famous contemporary, John Wesley, with his inflammatory remarks when it came to publicly decrying the evils of feasting, drinking, dancing, and indeed, most pastimes the locals enjoyed! He was never going to go down well in Hay, which in those days "was noted for wickedness".

An anonymous contemporary account takes up the story:

... For a while he was listened to in silence... but before his discourse was ended Satan began to rage in earnest... Stones were cast at him... one cowardly ruffian, standing behind the preacher, threw at him a huge stone, which, striking his head, caused him to fall senseless to the ground. He was carried to the inn where he was staying, and there died from the effects of the blow.

According to other sources, however, including Seward's own journal, this is an over-dramatic version of events. These tell of serious injuries not only inflicted at Hay but at other preaching stops along the way. Perhaps the injuries inflicted on Black Lion Green were the final straw. Seward was buried in Cusop churchyard, just a stone's throw from here, on the English side of the Dulas Brook.

A more light-hearted local story tells that whichever newly wed partner is the first to drink the water from Black Lion Well will have the upper hand in the marriage. A corresponding tale tells of the groom, who, leaving his new bride standing at the altar, rushed straight to the Well to drink the 'magic water'. However, when he got back to his wife and proudly told her what he had done, she pulled out an empty bottle, told him she had filled it the night before with well water, and had drunk it as soon as he had rushed off!

A stone with a blue plaque marks the site of the well, to the left of the path by the river (possibly hidden by parked cars).

Before leaving here, you might like to participate in one other local tradition, always popular with visitors. Walk onto the middle of the bridge over the Dulas and you'll have one foot in England, one foot in Wales!

*Return to the top of the hill and bear left until you emerge onto Lion Street by the **Old Black Lion** pub (see p113). Turn right and continue for a few yards past the pub to **The Hay Binders** (www.thehaybinders.co.uk) one of two bookbinders in town. Look in the window and if Christine is there she will be pleased to show you the work carried out there.*

*Retrace your steps a few yards and turn right into Bear Street, passing the **Old Stables Tea Rooms** (see p115) and the handsome half-timbered Bear, once a 16C coaching inn, before emerging back into the centre of town.*

For an optional short diversion (which leads to the main car park), turn left at Haywain Antiques and continue up the hill, past Hay Baptist Chapel, which includes a schoolroom that dates from 1647. Continue straight ahead.

The Black Mountains Bindery

This traditional bookbinders is run by Chris Bradshaw, who has three decades of experience in this age-old craft. You can watch him at work, lovingly restoring dog-eared, flappy-covered heirlooms back to gleaming 'as new' prized possessions. Chris is also a poet and edits Hay's biannual poetry magazine, *Quirk*, on sale here.

Open Tue–Sat 11am–5.30pm.

Turn right at the end of the road to the main car park, or return to the town centre.

Hay in Others' Words...

*Hay-on-Wye is **not about the books you are looking for: it's about the books that are looking for you.** It's a sanctuary for books you would never have thought of looking for in the first place.* Paul Collins, journalist.

*His [Richard Booth's] spoof independence movement struck a vein of Welsh independence, and tickled, too. Ever since, the inhabitants have found it impossible to keep straight faces. **In this magical town, sheep live in bottles and you can hear the sound of one hand clapping.*** John Windsor, journalist.

*The **unspeakable in search of the unreadable.*** An uncharitable description of bargain-book seekers by a former manager at one of Richard Booth's bookshops (which will remain anonymous!).

*The most important geographic feature of Hay is that it is **not near London.*** Richard Booth.

*I think of Hay-on-Wye as a place **standing at some slight angle to the rest of the known universe:** perhaps a sort of Brigadoon that isn't really there for the rest of the twelvemonth.* Christopher Hitchens, musing on whether the town really exists outside the Festival period.

*Young people really connect with images of real books and old books in particular, especially leather bindings, the classic Penguin and decorative cloth. It's totally different from buying online. **Make the place magic and the books choose you.*** Anne Brichto, co-owner of Addyman Books.

*Living in Hay is like being trapped in **a railway compartment full of escaped lunatics.*** Jonathan Meades, writer and filmmaker.

*A town **where the dustman talks like Freud.***
Dr Simon Nothman (associate of Richard Booth in the 1970s).

The ability of local entrepreneurs to connect with [the] idea of **'business-as-unusual'** *serves to cement the town's spirit of difference and dynamism.* Oliver Balch, author, journalist and Clyro local.

Books *£1.50 a carload,* **perfect for woodburning stoves.** Advertisement by Richard Booth in the Hay local paper, subsequently seized upon by the BBC Six O'Clock News and 'outraged' national press!

Hay isn't on the road to anywhere else. *There are no pylons in any direction. So to avoid disappearing from the map altogether, it decided to become a destination in itself.* Duncan Fallowell, *The Spectator.*

Hay is a market town, and it's whatever the market will bear. At one time it was sheep, it was butter, it was cheese, it was books. And now maybe **Hay is heading for the next thing, which could well be ideas.** Elizabeth Haycox, owner of Richard Booth's Bookshop.

I don't like the idea of being some kind of supernatural policeman! *Gods loves sinners and saints, the drunkard as much as the ascetic. Modern church life has the clergy sitting on committees or behind computer screens. I prefer to be about town 'loitering with divine intent'.* **Being a priest has a vulnerability** *which many people don't understand.* **They think you sit on a pedestal, but then so does a coconut!** Father Richard of St Mary's Church, proving that Hay attracts articulate humorous mavericks across every profession!

Hay has always been a weird place. You go back hundreds of years, and it's been **a magnet for eccentrics...** *There is a real spirit that runs through this place, and when you get that groundswell, it creates a snowball effect. When we left London, a lot of* **people said we would be bored in a backwater, but actually it's the opposite.** *Hay's a border town that takes inspiration from both sides. It's always changing.* Andrew Williams, co-owner Eighteen Rabbit, Hay.

Hay is **a small country town of the kind you can still find in France but which have almost disappeared in Britain.** *Most have become choked with traffic and buried in industrial and suburban development, but* **Hay is no bigger than in the 1870s** *when the diarist Francis Kilvert was curate in the next-door parish.* Ben Mallalieu, The *Guardian.*

The Great Outdoors

Hay has two wonderful natural features on its doorstep; the Brecon Beacons National Park, whose north-eastern tip lies just a 10-minute walk away from the centre of town, and the River Wye, which borders the town. So, put that book down, get outside and get some fresh air into your lungs!

Walking the Hills

The most spectacular and popular short walk near Hay, certainly with visitors, is the ascent of **Hay Bluff** (2,221ft/677m), the landmark peak that marks the northerly limit of the Black Mountains. While more serious walkers may set out from the town car park and walk the whole seven-plus miles (it's not so much the distance, as the gradient that is challenging), most visitors drive, via Forest Road, and park by the patch of land at the bottom of the Bluff; in good weather there's often an ice-cream van here! It's then a steep 20–25 minute climb to the top; hardly the Eiger, but a minimum level of fitness is required. If you have any breath left at this point, the views from up here *(see opp)* will take it clean away.

A mile or so south, on the same road, is **Twmpa** (aka Lord Hereford's Knob), another popular brisk ascent of similar height, (2,260 ft/690m), with a more droll name but a less punishing gradient. A third popular peak, which also rises just over 2000ft (600m) and boasts a terrific panorama, is the **Black Hill** (aka 'The Cat's Back').

All of these peaks fall within, or look onto the Brecon Beacons National Park, and exploring the magnificent landscapes of the Park on foot is a walker's paradise. Beware, though, the weather can change in a matter of minutes, so be prepared; fatalities, even among the SAS, who use the Beacons as a training ground, do occur.

Drover Holidays offer group guided walking tours with set departure dates and also offer tailormade, guided, half-day, full day or multi-day trips. *www.droverholidays.co.uk*

If you want to strike out on your own, the best source of advice is the Brecon Beacons National Park Visitor Centre, at Libanus, 35 miles southwest of Hay. *www.breconbeacons.org*

Long-distance paths and trails

Offa's Dyke Path, which follows the England–Wales border, and is named by *Lonely Planet* as 'one of the world's great walks', goes literally through the centre of town (albeit invisibly, as nothing now remains of the dyke). To the south of town, it runs alongside the main car park, out towards Cusop; on the north side, signposted at Hay Bridge, it runs along the north/west bank of the Wye for a short way, before heading towards Kington. For more on the walk, including its historical origins *(see p7)*.

In total, the Path runs for 177 miles (283km), but of course you don't need to walk it in one go, or carry your non-essential kit all the way, as the route can be broken down to manageable chunks, with various operators offering onward transport of luggage, accommodation en route, and other services. *www.offasdyke.org.uk.*

The lesser known **Wye Valley Walk**, covering 136 miles (218 km), crosses Offa's Dyke Path at Hay Bridge, and heads almost due west to Hereford. *www.wyevalleywalk.org.*

Get Kitted Out

Whatever you plan doing in the great outdoors around Hay, be prepared for the weather to change rapidly, dress accordingly, and take appropriate equipment, food and drink. Hay has two outdoors outfitters in **Golesworthys** *(see p67)* and **Rohan** on Castle Street. Golesworthys also stock a very good range of maps and local walking guides, as does the tourist office.

On Your Bike

Whether you fancy a gentle jaunt on an electric bike, a tandem for two, or you want to go the full Bradley Wiggins on a lung-bursting Lycra-clad adventure in the Brecon Beacons, you'll find all the equipment, route maps and advice you need at **Drover Cycles** on Forest Road, a five-minute walk from the main car park; *www.drovercycles.co.uk*. As well as all kinds of bikes for hire (and sale), they also have neat accessories for rent, such as cycle sat-navs. Drover can also deliver bikes to your accommodation, or choice of location, within a 20-mile radius.

From Forest Road, experienced cyclists can climb straight up (and we mean up) into the hills, past Hay Bluff, and over the stunning Gospel Pass, enjoying the views from the highest tarmac road in Wales, on towards Llanthony Priory *(see p103)*. There are also plenty of off-road mountain biking opportunities close by. Group guided tours are available with sister company, **Drover Holidays**, *www.droverholidays.co.uk*.

Mountain bikes and group guided tours are also on offer at Glasbury Bridge. *www.wyevalleycanoes.co.uk*.

Horse Riding

Tregoyd Mountain Riders, near Hay, offers horse riding and pony trekking for all ages, from beginners to advanced, for a half day, full day or more. You can ride straight out onto the open commons and hillsides of the Black Mountains, and stunning views of the river and the Wye Valley below, with the mountain ranges of the Brecon Beacon National Park as the backdrop. *www.tregoydriding.co.uk*

Another local operator, appealing to more experienced riders, though also catering for beginners, is **Freerein** in Clyro. They offer guided and unique bespoke self-guided riding holidays, exploring the hills around Hay, lasting from two to seven days. En route, you, and your mount, will stay in specially selected pubs, farms or guesthouses. Freerein accommodate beginners with three-day holidays. *www.free-rein.co.uk*

A River Runs Through It

The River Wye runs in total for 134 miles from mid-Wales to the Severn Estuary. The Hay stretch of the Wye meanders gently, between low grassy banks and tall trees, from Glasbury (*glaze-bury*) Bridge, five miles south-west, to Whitney-on-Wye Bridge, five miles north-east. En route it passes The Warren (*see p84*) and Hay Bridge.

If you haven't been in a canoe in a long time, or indeed ever, don't worry, as there are few barriers to enjoying a day on the river. It's very safe, child-friendly and suitable for all ages. All the operators mentioned below are experts on the water and will brief you thoroughly, including on what to bring and wear before you set out. And, unless you're experienced, you will always be part of a guided group so no need to worry about getting lost or falling in (which rarely happens!). All ready to paddle? First, choose from a Canadian canoe (think Native American Indian style, propelled by a single paddle) or a more sporty, single or double kayak (think Olympic whitewater canoe, with a double-bladed paddle). Second, decide how long you want to be out for. Half a day? A full day? Longer? If you want to channel your inner Steve Redgrave/Bear Grylls, you can take a four-or-five day/one-hundred-mile paddle from Glasbury to Chepstow. Whichever duration or distance, you only ever paddle *with* the current (downstream) and, if you're with a canoe hire operator you'll always be picked up and returned to your start point.

At any point on the river, keep your eyes peeled for herons, cormorants, swans, sand martins, herons, grebes and the electric-blue flash of a kingfisher. If you're lucky you may even see otters.

The closest canoe operator to the centre of town, and probably the best for novices and families, is the friendly well established team at **Want to Canoe?** *(pic below)* a five-minute walk across Hay Bridge. A good route for beginners is the half-day Hay to Whitney paddle, with an abundance of birdlife and (late in the year) leaping salmon. Another lovely half-day stretch is Bredwardine to Hereford. From picturesque red-brick Bredwardine Bridge, the river meanders past Brobury Scar – a high red sandstone cliff, clothed with beech woodland down to the

water's edge – on through the Georgian estate of Moccas Court, to Monnington and the falls at the National Trust Weir Gardens (don't panic, they are not overly challenging). If you can stretch to two or more days you can explore the most scenic and undisturbed parts of the Wye Valley, heading down through Hereford, Ross-on-Wye and Monmouth.

www.canoehire.co.uk; canoe-hire available every day, guided tours during school hols and most weekends.

Also in Hay, **PSM Outdoors** offers guided canoeing tours and courses. *www.psmoutdoors.co.uk.*

Glasbury hosts two good operators: **Celtic Canoes** *(www.celticcanoes.co.uk; summer only)* and **Wye Valley Canoes** *(www.wyevalleycanoes.co.uk; year round).*

Do it all!

There are two multi-activity outdoor adventures companies just outside Hay. At Llanigon is **Outdoors@Hay** who offer a smorgasbord of canoeing, raft building, gorge walking (*pic above*), mountain biking, bushcraft, archery, orienteering, climbing and abseiling, *www.outdoorsathay.com*. At Glasbury is **Interactivities**, who offer caving, hill walking, canoeing, raft building, gorge walking and two less usual activities: combat archery ('paintballing with bows and arrows') and mountain boarding ('snowboarding meets skateboarding'). *www.interactivities-uk.com*.

Fishing

Coarse fishing is excellent on the Hay stretch of the Wye, the main species being barbel, pike and chub, with roach, perch, bream and dace also occasionally caught. Bredwardine is renowned for game fishing, with large numbers of salmon and trout. Fishing is not permitted anywhere on the Wye without a licence; ask at Golesworthys in Hay or visit *www.haywarren.org.uk*.

TO THE GLORY OF GOD
AND IN PROUD AND HONOURED
MEMORY OF
CAPT RALPH HOPTON BASKERVILLE.
CORP! WILLIAM C. ROBERTS.
PTE FRANCIS H. ANTHONY,
WILLIAM F. FRY,
ALBERT HARRIS,

Half an Hour from Hay

One of the most important factors in determining Hay's character over the years has been its isolation. For better or for worse, main roads bypass it and the railway left town nearly 60 years ago. That said, if you are staying here for a few days and want to see more of the Marches, there are plenty of interesting places to visit nearby.

Clyro

Just over a mile from Hay, across the Wye, this small village boasts ties with two writers: one internationally famous, one locally famous.

The Victorian clergyman, **Reverend Francis Kilvert**, lived here from 1868–1875 and his diaries from this period provide a vibrant insight into rural life in the High Victorian period. What Pepys was to London, Kilvert was to Hay and its surrounding villages. Like Pepys, he was prolific with the pen, and also had an eye for the ladies – a trait that was to indirectly undermine his legacy. It is reckoned that in total, Kilvert may have written up to a million words about the area, but sadly much of this was destroyed, after his death, by his widow, because (it is assumed) she did not wish details of his relationships with other women to be published. Enough remains, however, to paint a vivid picture of local life.

In the centre of Clyro, opposite Kilvert's handsome former home, stands the **Baskerville Arms** pub. Above its door is a black dog, representing the Hound of the Baskervilles. Why here? According to the owners of **Baskerville Hall**, a great rambling 19C pile, now a hotel, just a short walk away (see p102), Sir Arthur Conan Doyle was a friend of the Baskerville family, visited here regularly and took inspiration from the vicious hounds of a particularly nasty local landowner, 'Black Vaughan'. It is said his dogs roamed the moors of nearby Hergest Ridge (see p104) and killed more than one 'trespasser'. So, why is the published story set on Dartmoor as opposed to in the Welsh Marches? Baskerville Hall claim that their ancestors did not want publicity and in fact wanted "to ward off tourists". Kilvert shared the same sense of antipathy; "of all noxious animals...the most noxious is a tourist", he wrote, blissfully unaware that one day *he* would become a tourist attraction. Or perhaps the story is set in Devon because Conan Doyle never visited the Welsh Marches while writing the story, as other credible sources claim. You can learn more about Kilvert, Clyro and Conan Doyle in the very good company of Hay Tours. *www.haytours.org.*

Baskerville Hall and The Story of Books

Based at Baskerville Hall, The Story of Books is an initiative led by Clyro-resident, Emma Balch, to create a new style of working museum dedicated to all aspects of books. At the heart of this is a collection of printing presses, and tools for papermaking and bookbinding, that will be put into daily working use. The Story of Books will also be producing exhibitions, theatrical performances, and live jazz, as part of an entertaining programme of events. It also has a presence at 20 Castle Street (next to The Great English Outdoors shop, *see p30*), where volunteers will be building 'The Clyro Press', a wooden rolling press based on a 17C illustration in Jan Luyken's *Book of Trades* (1694). For details of opening times, exhibitions and events at both venues, see *www.thestoryofbooks.com*.

Baskerville Hall is host to several music events and festivals throughout the year, including Hay Festival Club Nights *(see p22)*. *www.baskervillehall.co.uk*.

Bridge on the River Wye

The easy way to get to Clyro is via Hay Bridge. You can return a different way however, by heading some four miles down the A438 (towards Hereford), then turning right, to cross the river over the picturesque wood-and-stone **Whitney Bridge**. Built in 1774, it is one of only eight privately owned toll bridges left in the UK, and today costs £1 to cross by motor vehicle. *www.whitneybridge.co.uk*

Capel-y-Ffinn and Llanthony Priory

Take Forest Road out of Hay, follow your nose, miles (25 mins) you will go through **Capel-y-Ffi** the boundary). It is famous for its tiny chapel ar road, its monastery, built in 1870 by 'Father Ign of restoring monastic life to the Church of Englan around 40 years. In 1924, it was bought by stone and typeface designer, Eric Gill, who lived here for ı ⹁day it is home to self-catering accommodation. The dr ⹁ ⹁o get here, winding through the Brecon Beacons, traversing the **Gospel Pass** – the highest public road in Wales (1801 ft/549m) – offers views that, even in this topographical delight, are breathtaking. Continue on the same road for another 3.6 miles.

The evocative ruins of **Llanthony Priory** represents one of the great buildings of medieval Wales, but it is also its situation, in the beautiful Vale of Ewyas *(you-us)*, in the shadow of the Black Mountains, that makes this such a special place.

The original Augustinian building was completely destroyed in the 12C and the ruins you see today are those of the 13C priory. Part of this has been renovated and integrated into the Llanthony Priory Hotel, where you can get lunch (book ahead), or just drop into its cellar bar, part of the original 12C priory, for a drink. *www.llanthonyprioryhotel.co.uk/the-history.*

Although the Priory is less than 12 miles from Hay, the journey is mostly on winding single track roads, with limited passing places, and takes around 40 minutes. Be prepared to give way at any time and to have to reverse – it's not for the faint-hearted or impatient, but it is well worthwhile.

...all market town, on the Black and White Trail *(see opposite)*, ...ddles the English-Welsh border and sits immediately below Hergest *(har-guest)* Ridge. From the centre of Kington, it's a 30-45 minute walk, along the Offa's Dyke Path *(see p94)* to the top of the ridge, marked by a clump of monkey puzzle trees. It may only be a modest 1398ft (426m) but offers magnificent 360-degree panoramas. Why the monkey puzzle trees? One story goes that they were planted by a gardener who noticed that the Ridge's winter climate closely resembled that of their native Patagonia. En route you'll pass **Hergest Croft Gardens**, famed for its rare plants, shrubs and trees, with over 90 'Champion Trees' (the largest of their species in the British Isles). *www.hergest.co.uk.*

Kington is also host to two walking festivals *(Apr and Sept)* and a large food festival *(Dec)*. Tourist office, 5 Church Street. *www.kingtontourist.info.*

Just out of town are two worthwhile excursions: the **Small Breeds Farm Park and Owl Centre** *(www.owlcentre.com)*, and **Westonbury Mill Water Gardens**, famous for its follies. *www.westonburymillwatergardens.com.*

Hergest Ridge

Music fans may know this as the name of Mike Oldfield's second album. The brilliant multi-instrumentalist was a resident of the area during the writing and recording of *Hergest Ridge*. Bizarrely, although this now largely forgotten album was released in 1974, over a year after Oldfield's multi-million selling *Tubular Bells*, it reached No. 1 in the album charts before his tour de force, and was only knocked off its perch by... *Tubular Bells*.

The Black and White Trail

This tourist route takes in the prettiest 'black-and-white' villages and towns in north-west Herefordshire; the name derives from the black-and-white half-timbered late-medieval houses.

Those closest to Hay are Eardisley, Kington *(see opposite)*, Dilwyn, Weobley *(webb-lee)*, Pembridge and Eardisland. Picture-postcard **Eardisland** boasts an extraordinary Georgian dovecote; in **Pembridge** don't pass the Old Chapel Gallery *(www.oldchapelgallery. co.uk)* or the striking medieval church; **Weobley** *(pic below)* is one of the best preserved Tudor villages in the whole country, also boasting a superb church with a 185-ft tall landmark 14C spire. *www.weobley.org.*

Most of the villages offer a choice of eating and drinking with at least one good pub, a café and/or restaurant. *www.blackandwhitetrail.org*

Brecon

The small town of Brecon is best known as the gateway to the **Brecon Beacons National Park**, though to experience its wide open spaces, it's best to drive another 15 minutes southwest to the main information office at Libanus (*www.breconbeacons. org*). There are wonderful views from here and a choice of walks to suit all. The big draw for reasonably fit walkers is Pen-y-Fan (*pic opposite*), which, at 2,907ft (886m), is not only the highest peak in the National Park, but the highest British peak south of Snowdonia. If you do want to tackle this, it's best to set out from the Pont ar Daf car park, by The Storey Arms, another 10 minutes south by car from Libanus. Whatever your plans, consult the staff at Libanus first.

Brecon is also famous for its **Jazz Festival**, founded in 1984, which once hosted some of the finest jazz musicians in the world. Today it is much smaller, and takes place over a long weekend in August, staging many free family-friendly events, including a carnival parade, in various venues around the town. *www.breconjazz.org*

From the pretty canal basin, Dragon Fly Cruises offer **boat hire and narrow-boat excursions**. From here you can cruise along the picturesque Monmouthshire and Brecon Canal, which hugs the mountainside above the valley of the River Usk. *www.dragonfly-cruises.co.uk*.

Crickhowell

Set in a beautiful part of the Brecon Beacons National Park, on the banks of the River Usk, with some of the Park's most popular peaks looking down upon it, this pretty little town (population 2,000) has much in common with Hay. It too is locally famous for its independent family-run shops and businesses, its strong community spirit, and it is also a festival town. There's a week-long Literary Festival (*Oct*), a nine-day **Walking Festival** (*late Feb–early Mar*) plus the **Green Man Festival** (*Aug*), one of the highlights of the UK music calendar. Tourist office (CRiC), Beaufort Street – *www.visitcrickhowell.co.uk*.

En route to Crickhowell from Hay, is sleepy **Talgarth**, home to **Talgarth Mill**, a meticulously restored 18C watermill with an excellent café, serving locally sourced food, including bread and cakes made from home-milled flour. Tours of the mill run six days a week, though the mill is usually only working three or four days a week, so call ahead. *www.talgarthmill.com, closed Mon*. Tourist office, The Square. *www.visittalgarth.co.uk*.

Eating Out

Two highly acclaimed restaurants that you might like to consider when you are out and about, are **The River Café** at Glasbury, just south of Hay (*www.wyevalleycanoes.co.uk*), and **The Felin Fach Griffin** (*www.eatdrinksleep.ltd.uk*), between Hay and Brecon.

Hereford

The main attraction of the county town is **Hereford Cathedral**, with its famous **Mappa Mundi**. Made c1300, this is the largest medieval map still in existence (5ft 2in x 4ft 4in/1.59 x 1.34m), and illustrates the history, geography and destiny of humanity as it was understood in Christian Europe, in the late 13C/early14C. The Cathedral's **Chained Library** is the largest survivor of its kind in the world with books and chains intact, and is home to one of just four copies of the 1217 version of Magna Carta. The statue of a resting cyclist outside the cathedral depicts the great composer, Sir Edward Elgar, who lived in Hereford 1904–1912. *www.herefordcathedral.org*

The history of the county's famous black-and-white houses is very well presented in **The Black and White House Museum**, a picture-postcard three-storey 17C timber-framed house, marooned amid a sea of modern mediocrity in the town centre. **Church Street**, a pedestrianised lane which runs between the commercial centre of town and the Cathedral, is another picturesque survivor of old Hereford, lined with independent shops and places to eat and drink. *www.churchstreethereford.co.uk*.

A 10-minute walk from the centre is the popular **Cider Museum**, showcasing the county's favourite tipple. *www.cidermuseum.co.uk.*

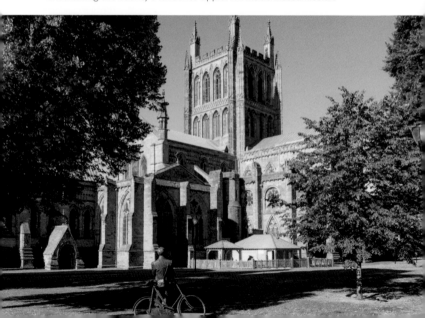

Erwood Station Gallery

If you like The Lion Street Gallery *(see p53)* and/or The Hay Makers Gallery *(see p59)*, you'll also like Erwood Station Gallery, enjoying a verdant setting by the River Wye, a 20-minute drive west of Hay. It is owned by Christina and Brent Blair, of Hay's Lion Street Gallery. Housed in a former railway station, including three carriages from the 1870s, the gallery features applied art and contemporary crafts across a wide range of media: ceramics, glass, jewellery, painting, metal, paper, wood and sculpture (the latter for home and garden). There's also a tearoom, a riverside walk and a restored locomotive.

www.erwoodstation.com. Open daily (closed 24 Dec–first week Feb).

Further Afield: Town and Country

Ludlow is an attractive, thriving market town, boasting some of the finest Georgian and half-timbered architecture in the country. The town has a lively community feel, excellent independent shops, a reputation for fine food, and is busy with markets, events and festivals throughout the year. Slap bang in the centre of town, visit its ruined medieval castle and Dinham House. *www.ludlow.org.uk*

The **Elan Valley** *(pic above)* is famous for its dams and reservoirs, built a hundred years ago in an epic feat of civil engineering to supply clean water to Birmingham. Set within an area of outstanding scenic beauty, it is a walker's paradise. *www.elanvalley.org.uk*

Both destinations are within an hour's drive of Hay.

Where to Eat and Drink

All of the establishments below pride themselves on a menu that is exclusively or mostly homemade, using fresh local ingredients wherever possible.

Opening times may be extended during Hay Festival (when booking ahead is vital).

What Other People Think: Rating as at end Feb 2018 (TripAdvisor, Facebook). No rating given if major recent changes.

The Globe at Hay Kitchen

Décor: 'Cheery industrial'

Type of Food: Snacks and burgers to Modern British/Welsh dishes.

Sample dishes: Slow cooked pork roulade stuffed with spinach, wild mushroom & ricotta cheese, crackling, with brandy, thyme & shallot sauce; Sweet pointed peppers stuffed with green pesto, new potatoes, feta cheese topped with toasted pine kernels.

Why/when to go: before a performance in The Globe *(see p72)* upstairs; Sunday lunch; look online for special deals.

What Other People Think: TripAdvisor 4.5 out of 5. 44 reviews. 89% Excellent/very good.

www.globeathay.org. Open lunch Wed–Sun; dinner 7pm–9pm Tues & Thu–Sat.

Red Indigo

Décor: 'Modern Asian'

Type of Food: Indian.

Sample dishes: go for the fenugreek flavoured Prema Rasayana, the sizzling tangy Lababdar, or the garlic chilli massala.

Why/when to go: if it's good enough for Jack Dee, Christine Brinkley, Ralph Fiennes, Clare Balding, Will Young...

What Other People Think: TripAdvisor 4 out of 5. 343 reviews. 80% Excellent/very good.

www.redindigo.co.uk. Open daily lunch and dinner.

St John's Place *(see p55)*

Décor: Modern-minimalist in former chapel

Type of Food: bang-on-trend, constantly changing menu.

Sample dishes: Fried chicken, kimchi, samphire & sesame; Hogget shoulder, carrots, turnips, greens & horseradish; Jerusalem artichoke & chestnut pie, pumpkin & sage.

Why/when to go: to impress, in a minimalist foodie kind of way.

What Other People Think: TripAdvisor 5 out of 5. 166 reviews. 98% Excellent/very good.

www.stjohnsplacehay.tumblr.com. Open Fri & Sat only, from 6pm. Booking essential at all times.

Note: During Hay Festival St John's Place is home to **A Rule of Tum** www.aruleoftum.com.

The Swan Hotel

Décor: Georgian elegance in Garden Room; Cosy lounge in 1812 Bar; Pub-like Market Bar.

Type of Food: Modern British/Welsh fine food.

Sample dishes: Tempura vegetables with Thai dipping sauce; Prime Welsh sirloin or rib-eye steak plus choice of sauces, Slow roasted lamb shank with sweet potato purée. Pie (of the day) & mash.

Why/when to go: top chef's cooking at pub prices; summer in the garden; cocktail happy hour (5–8pm); Pudding Nights (last Wed of month); special occasions. Afternoon Tea Mon–Sat 3–5pm.

www.swanathay.com. Open daily.

Pubs and Bars

Beer Revolution *(see p51)*

Décor: 'Industrial-warehouse'

Type of food: 'goes-well-with-a-beer' snacks.

Sample dishes: Cuban sandwiches, gourmet hot dogs, pizzas, quesadillas, Totally Welsh Rarebit.

Why/when to go: Best range of beers in Hay and far beyond; summer 'secret garden'.

What Other People Think: Facebook 4.9 out of 5. 37 reviews.

www.beerrevolution.co.uk; Open Mon–Thur 10am–5pm, Fri–Sat 10am–10pm, Sun 12–5pm (food served Fri & Sat noon–9pm).

The Blue Boar

Décor/Atmosphere: 'Hay hygge', a Hay institution.

Type of Food: superior pub grub.

Sample dishes: Game pie, Glamorgan (vegetarian) sausages, lasagne.

Why/when/where to go: summer in the 'secret' courtyard garden, winter by the open fires.

What Other People Think: TripAdvisor 4 out of 5. 619 reviews. 74% Excellent/very good.

Open daily.

The Hay Tap at Kilverts Hotel (see p53)

(see p53)

Décor: Traditional pub.

Type of Food/Drink: hearty pies for carnivores and vegetarians. Excellent range of drinks.

Sample dishes: Steak & ale pie; chicken & Perl Las pie; mushroom, kale & chestnut pie.

Why/when to go: Pie & a pint. Front terrace for people watching, large back garden in summer, open fire in winter.

What Other People Think: TripAdvisor 4 out of 5. 189 reviews. 69% Excellent/very good.

www.kilverts.co.uk. Open daily.

The Old Black Lion

Décor: Cosy 17C beamed Olde English pub.

Type of Food/Drink: British/Italian.

Sample dishes: Local lamb chops with roast crushed potatoes & balsamic jus; Pan-fried fillet of cod, new potatoes, with kale & citrus salsa.

Why/when to go: Friday night jazz (booking essential).

What Other People Think: TripAdvisor 4.5 out of 5. 318 reviews. 86% Excellent/very good.

www.oldblacklion.co.uk Open lunch and dinner daily.

Tomatitos Tapas Bar *(see p55)*

Décor: Stylish modern renovation of beamed pub.

Type of Food/Drink: Authentic tapas. Good value Spanish wine.

Sample dishes: Chorizo cooked in cider, *albondigas* (pork & herb meatballs), *Gratinada de verdura de temporada* (seasonal vegetables slow cooked with tomatoes & herbs, gratiné).

Why/when to go: Anytime, including morning coffee – nearly always busy (no bookings less than parties of 8). Open fire in winter.

What Other People Think: TripAdvisor 4.5 out of 5. 650 reviews. 92% Excellent/very good.

www.haytomatitos.co.uk. Open daily.

Daytime only

Eve's

Décor: Cheery Modern (inc. clothing accessories shop).

Type of Food: cakes, sandwiches, toasties.

Why/when to go: the coffee; consistently lovely staff; people watching on front 'grass' terrace.

What Other People Think: TripAdvisor 4.5 out of 5. 94 reviews. 87% Excellent/very good.

Open daily.

The Granary *(see p67)*

Décor: Rustic former early 19C grain store.

Type of Food: Snacks, soups, salads, Sunday roast. Plenty of vegetarian choices.

Why/when to go: Summer to sit on the terrace and watch the to-ings and fro-ings; winter by the open fire.

What Other People Think: TripAdvisor 4 out of 5. 502 reviews. 71% Excellent/very good.

Open daily.

The Old Electric Shop *(see p68)*

Décor: Vintage/on-trend.

Type of Food: Vegetarian and vegan meals and soups.

Sample dishes: Buddha bowl, Lebanese platter, Persian stew.

Why/when to go: the coffee; 'Hay's hippest café' *(Lonely Planet)*; play chess while you eat; vintage browsing; during festivals.

What Other People Think: TripAdvisor 4.5 out of 5. 98 reviews. 89% Excellent/very good.

www.oldelectric.co.uk. Open daily.

The Old Stables Tea Rooms

Décor: Old-fashioned, vintage, cosy.

Type of Food: Welsh steak & ale Pie, Welsh Rarebit, grilled salmon fillet with a whisky cream sauce. Whimberry & apple pie. Cream Teas, speciality teas. Award-winning cakes, jams and marmalades.

Why/when to go: *Best Tea/Coffee Shop* at Welsh Regional Awards 2016. Summer to sit outdoors.

What Other People Think: TripAdvisor 4.5 out of 5. 146 reviews. 86% Excellent/very good.

www.oldstablestearooms.co.uk. Open Tue–Sat noon–3pm Closed mid-Dec–Easter.

Oscar's Bistro

Décor: Stripped wood (more café than bistro).

Type of Food: Soup, paninis, quiche & salad, German apple cake, carrot cake.

Why/when to go: Summer when the tables spill out onto the streets.

What Other People Think: TripAdvisor 3.5 out of 5. 296 reviews. 55% Excellent/very good.

Open daily.

Richard Booth's Bookshop Café

Décor: Light, contemporary, airy, flagstone floors, arty posters, outdoor courtyard.

Sample dishes: Devilled portobello mushroom & fried egg on sourdough toast; Smoked haddock fish cakes, tartar sauce, crunchy slaw.

Why/when to go: Summer to sit outdoors. Sunday brunch. Creative cooking. Getting lost in books before and after (see p63). The coffee.

What Other People Think: TripAdvisor 4.5 out of 5. 402 reviews. 88% Excellent/very good

www.boothbooks.co.uk. Open Tue–Sun.

Shepherds Ice Cream Parlour (see p42)

Décor: Former fishmongers with original tiling.

Type of Food: Ice cream sundaes and shakes, ice-cream and hot waffles. Cakes, patisserie, paninis and sandwiches.

Why/when to go: Ice cream treats in summer, hearty home-made vegetable soup in winter. Sit inside by the full-length front window or outside on the terrace and watch Hay go by.

What Other People Think: TripAdvisor 4.5 out of 5. 250 reviews. 86% Excellent/very good.

www.shepherdsicecream.co.uk. Open daily.

Take Away/Eat-in

The Salad Project

Décor: 'Hole-in-the-wall', but seating for 5 people.

Type of Food: 100% vegetarian. Summer: falafels, quesadillas, halloumi, houmous and super colourful salads. Winter: warming curries, stews, homemade flatbreads.

What Other People Think: TripAdvisor 5 out of 5. 26 reviews. 100% Excellent.

Open Wed–Sat 11.30–2ish.

THE START
RIVERSIDE
B & B
01497 821391
E-mail: dawn@the-start.net

NO VACANCIES

Getting to Hay by Public Transport

The nearest mainline railway station to Hay is Hereford, 20 miles east. The no39 bus service runs from here, Monday through Saturday, through the Golden Valley, taking just over an hour to get to Hay. Pick up a timetable at Hay Tourist Office or look online for details. The same service continues from Hay on to Brecon (42 mins), but there is no railway station at Brecon.

On Sundays and bank holiday Mondays, the Hay Ho! bus runs the same route, but take note that the last bus leaves Hereford at 16.10. This service is also useful to walkers; eg. if you alight at Dorstone you can walk the eight miles back to Hay, via Arthur's Stone, following the Herefordshire Trail and Wye Valley Walk. *www.hayhobus.org.uk*

If you are coming from Cardiff, the fastest way to Hay is by train to Hereford (63-88 mins), then the no39 or the Hay Ho! Bus.

During Hay Festival, there is a more direct Festival Link Bus service to Hereford, as well as a service to Worcester. *www.hayfestival.com*

If you are staying at Clyro or nearby, on the north side of the Wye, catch the X15 Hereford to Builth Wells bus, which takes just over 40 minutes to Clyro.

Visitor Information

On arrival in Hay, make sure you call at the friendly and helpful Tourist Information Bureau, across the road from the Oxford Road car park. Open Mon–Sat: 10am–4.30pm, Sun 11am–3pm Easter/April through September; reduced hours rest of the year.

Hay Online

www.hay-on-wye.co.uk The official website for visitors.
www.visithay.co.uk A private initiative, also aimed at visitors.
www.eatsleepliveherefordshire.co.uk What's happening in Herefordshire.
www.lifeinhay.blogspot.co.uk A local's diary of everyday life in Hay.
www.hayhistorygroup.co.uk Hay History
www.haytours.org Hay Tours

Opening Times

Shop opening times *(see front inside flap)*.

Where to Stay in Hay

There are literally hundreds of accommodation providers in and around Hay, from modest single-room B&Bs to grand stately-like homes and luxury converted barns, designed to take large parties. In Hay itself, The Swan is the only bona-fide hotel. Pubs and bars that offer accommodation in Hay are Kilverts Hotel, The Old Black Lion and Tomatitos. Just outside Hay (1.6 miles) is the Baskerville Hall Hotel.

If you're planning to visit during the Festival, you need to book as far in advance as possible; *www.visithay.co.uk* is the official accommodation service and booking agent for the Festival.

For a list of all accommodations approved by the Hay tourist office, visit *www.hay-on-wye.co.uk/accommodation*. This is not to say that other accommodations are not worth considering; however, it is not within the scope of this guide to make recommendations.

What's on in and Around Hay

Calendar of events

Jan Wassailing. *www.eatsleepliveherefordshire.co.uk*

Late Feb–Mar Borderlines Film Festival. *www.borderlinesfilmfestival.co.uk* Crickhowell Walking Festival. *www.crickhowellfestival.com*

Apr Independence Celebrations. Hay (Chamber) Music Festival *(see p63, p82)*. Kington Walks Spring Festival. *www.kingtonwalks.org*

May Talgarth Walking Festival. *www.talgarthwalkingfestival.org*

Late May–early Jun Hay Festival *(see p19-p27)*. HowTheLightGetsIn *(see p74-p75)*. Hay Fair on the Square. *www.hay-on-wye.co.uk/info/events.asp*

Jun Herefordshire Walking Festival. *www.walkingfestival.com*

Jul Royal Welsh Show, Builth Wells. *www.rwas.wales* Hay-on-Wye Horse Show. *www.hayhorseshow.co.uk*

Aug Vintage Steam & Vintage Rally. *www.vintage-society.org* Brecon Jazz Festival *(see p106)*. Truefest, Clyro. *www.truefest.co.uk*

Sep Herefordshire Art Week. *www.h-art.org.uk*

Nov Hay Winter Weekend *(see p26)*.

Dec Christmas shop window dressing competition. Kington Food Festival *(see p104)*.

Regular Weekly Events/Meetings

Events below held at The Globe (*www.globeathay.org/whats-on*) unless otherwise stated.

Tue Open Mic Night every week, Chess first and third Tuesday of month, Death Café (tackling the complex ideas that surround death) second Tuesday of month, Science Café fourth Tuesday of month.

Wed Acoustic Music night at Baskerville Hall Hotel, Clyro.

Thur Philosophy Café (every other week).

Fri. Let's Get Quizzical (first Fri of month) or live music at The Globe. Jazz at the Old Black Lion (*see p113*).

Sat Live music at The Globe (*pic below*); Hay Jazz live at St Mary's Church (monthly Apr-Sept).

Sun Lego Club 11am.

Richard Booth's Bookshop Cinema screens films and live events (from the ROH, NT etc.) most nights. *www.boothbooks.co.uk*.

Broad Sheep is an excellent comprehensive free listings magazine covering Herefordshire and the Marches, while **Wye Local** is a free local magazine, covering Hay, Talgarth and surrounding villages, that also includes what's on information. Both are available in cafés, pubs, music venues and online. *www.broadsheep.com*.

For more information visit Hay Tourist Information Bureau.

www.hay-on-wye.co.uk/info/events.asp.

Further Reading

Local History

The Book of Hay by Kate Clake with Clare Purcell and Mari Fforde. The history of Hay.

Old Hay in pictures and prints by Eric Pugh. An archive of black-and-white Hay photos, going back to the 19th century.

The Town of Hay – Then and Now by Eric & Tim Pugh. Contemporary photos rub shoulders with historic shots.

The Hay Poisoner by Martin Beales. *(see p70-71).*

Kilvert's Diary by Reverend Francis Kilvert *(see p101).*

Local Photo Essays and Illustrated Books

Hay Landscape, Literature and the Town of Books by Jim Saunders. Hay and the surrounding area, with some fine landscape photography.

Planet Hay by Huw Parsons. An evocative look back at Hay over the last 30 years or so, with the emphasis on its colourful local characters.

O Happy Hay! by Eugene Fisk. A charming illustrated personal take on Hay, by a local artist.

Non-Fiction

My Kingdom of Books by Richard Booth. The often-amusing and engagingly self-deprecating autobiography of the King of Hay.

Sixpence House by Paul Collins. An American writer arrives in Hay in the late 1990s, looking for a home.

Under the Tump by Oliver Balch. Astute sketches of contemporary local life from a travel writer and journalist, seeking to assimilate in present-day Hay.

Fiction

Addlands by Tom Bullough. A sweeping tale of the hardships of one family, from World War II to the present day, set in the Radnorshire Hills.

Lady of Hay by Barbara Erskine *(see p39).*

The Magus of Hay by Phil Rickman *(see p39).*

On the Black Hill by Bruce Chatwin *(see p69).*

Resistance by Owen Sheers. An alternative history novel, set in 1944–45, in a valley near Abergavenny, in the wake of a German invasion.

Thank you, thank you , thank you!

To the following people who, in one way or another, have made this book possible. Thank you to all the team at Orphans Press, Kitty Corrigan, Clare Fry, Andrew Williams, Anne Brichto, Alan Nicholls, Mari Fforde, Gareth Howell-Jones, Emily Daw, Huw Parsons, The Swan Hotel, Cusop History Group and all the shopkeepers and businesses in Hay who have been so generous with their time and assistance.

And of course, thank you to Richard Booth and Peter Florence, without whom Hay would have been a very different, and probably much less interesting place.

Finally my apologies to anyone whose business is not included in this guide; there is simply not enough space here for everybody. Look out for the next edition.

Photo and Artwork Credits

Cover Design, Layout and Maps: Orphans.co.uk

Maps reproduced by kind permission: Derek Glashan of Hay Deli (town map); Eric and Tim Pugh (riverside map).

The following photographers and businesses gave their kind permission for use of these images: p6 Myrabella (Wikimedia Commons); p8, p56 (bottom middle) Jasper Fforde; p14 (r) Tom Ordelman; p16 Nexxo (Wikimedia Commons); pp18, p24 (r) Sam J Peat; p20 Hay Festival; p22 Aaron Marcus Sutton; p23 Sam Hardwick; p24 (l) Michael Howles; p26 Hay Food Festival 2015 (photographer unknown); p27 (above) Daniel Mordzinski; p31 Jacqueline Kennett; pp34 Wikimedia Commons, by Samuel Ireland (d. 1800); p 37 (above) Wikimedia Commons, by John George Wood (1768–1838); p39 Phil Rickman; p42 Shepherds Ice Cream; p44 100% Hay; p61 The Table; p62 (bottom left) Hay Festival 2017; p64 (above) Hay Festival; p65 Martin Walker; p70 Alan Duncan; p74 Jenna Foxton (IAI/ HTLGI); p75 (far l and far r) Justine Trickett (IAI/ HTLGI); p81 John Symonds; p82 (l) Nicholas de Jong Cleyndert (r) Huw Parsons; p83 Nic the Computer Guy; p85 Eric Pugh; p95 Freerein Riding Holidays; p99 Outdoors@Hay; p107 Visit Wales Image Centre; p108 Alex Ramsay.

All other photographs in this book have been taken by the author. No part of this book may be used or reproduced in any format without the prior permission of the author.

Index